Disclaimer

All erudition contained in this book is given for informational and educational purposes
only. The author is not in any way accountable for any results or outcomes that emanate
from using this material. Constructive attempts have been made to
provide information that is both accurate and effective, but the author is not bound for
the accuracy or use/misuse of this information.

Meditations

The Diary of Marcus Aurelius - Memories, Thoughts and Reflections - The Stoic Philosophy of the Greatest Roman Emperor

Marcus Aurelius and Julius A. Klein

Contents

Book I

In recounting the life and lessons of Marcus Aurelius, one is struck by the profound influence of his familial lineage and the myriad mentors who sculpted the bedrock of his character.

From his esteemed grandfather, Verus, Marcus learned the virtues of moral rectitude and temperance in governance, foundational principles that fortified his ethical bearings.

The paternal legacy, embodied by his father, Marcus learnt a deep sense of dignity and propriety. These early influences served as guiding beacons in his formative years.

From his father, Marcus Aurelius saw and took up a great deal of virtues and traits. His father was mild-mannered, resolute after thorough consideration, modest while receiving honors, had a strong work ethic, and was receptive to advice for the sake of the group. He was unwaveringly fair in treating individuals based solely on their merits, he knew when to act vigorously and when to exercise caution, and he never allowed flattery or popularity to cloud his judgment.

Marcus saw in his father a careful investigation of issues before drawing conclusions, fidelity in friendships without ostentation, foresight and provision for necessities without ostentation, and moderation in the use of life's comforts without conceit or justifications. He was well-liked for being a mature, unattractive person who knew how to handle both private and public matters.

His father conversed amiably and unpretentiously, avoided criticism and was not easily swayed by imposters, and valued real philosophers. He complied with his nation's standards without pretense, took reasonable, not excessive, care of his health, and freely supported the abilities of others.

Marcus wrote;

From my governor, to be neither of the green nor of the blue party at the games in the Circus, nor a partizan either of the Parmularius or the Scutarius at the gladiators' fights; from him too I learned endurance of labour, and to want little, and to work with my own hands, and not to meddle with other people's affairs, and not to be ready to listen to slander.

From Fronto I learned to observe what envy, and duplicity, and hypocrisy are in a tyrant, and that generally those among us who are called Patricians are rather deficient in paternal affection.

From Alexander the Platonic, not frequently nor without necessity to say to any one, or to write in a letter, that I have no leisure; nor continually to excuse the neglect of duties required by our relation to those with whom we live, by alleging urgent occupations.

From Catullus, not to be indifferent when a friend finds fault, even if he should find fault without reason, but to try to restore him to his usual disposition; and to be ready to speak well of teachers, as it is reported of Domitius and Athenodotus; and to love my children truly.

From my brother Severus, to love my kin, and to love truth, and to love justice; and through him I learned to know Thrasea, Helvidius, Cato, Dion, Brutus; and from him I received the idea of a polity in which there is the same law for all, a polity administered with regard to equal rights and equal freedom of speech, and the idea of a kingly government which respects most of all the freedom of the governed; I learned from him also consistency and undeviating steadiness in my regard for philosophy; and a disposition to do good, and to give to others readily, and to cherish good hopes, and to believe that I am loved by my friends; and in him I observed no concealment of his opinions with respect to those whom he condemned, and that his friends had no need to conjecture what he wished or did not wish, but it was quite plain.

From Maximus I learned self-government, and not to be led aside by anything; and cheerfulness in all circumstances, as well as in illness; and a just admixture in the moral character of sweetness and dignity, and to do what was set before me without complaining. I observed that everybody believed that he thought as he spoke, and that in all that he did he never had any bad intention; and he never showed amazement and surprise, and was never in a hurry, and never put off doing a thing, nor was perplexed nor dejected, nor did he ever laugh to disguise his vexation, nor, on the other hand, was he ever passionate or suspicious. He was accustomed to do acts of beneficence, and was ready to forgive, and was free from all falsehood; and he presented the appearance of a man who could not be diverted from right rather than of a man who had been improved.

8

I observed, too, that no man could ever think that he was despised by Maximus, or ever venture to think himself a better man. He had also the art of being humorous in a pleasant way.

At the end of the writings of what he learnt from each personality figure, Marcus Aurelius expressed deep gratitude towards the gods for various blessings in his life.

Book II

It contains reflections on the transitory nature of life and the importance of living according to reason and virtue.

Begin the morning by saying to thyself, I shall meet with the busy-body, the ungrateful, arrogant, deceitful, envious, unsocial.

They experience all of these things as a result of their lack of moral awareness. But since I've witnessed the ugly and beautiful aspects of both good and bad, as well as the similarity between wrongdoing and myself in terms of shared intelligence and a portion of divinity, I am unable to be hurt by any of them. No one can find anything ugly about me, and I am also unable to feel hate or anger toward my kinsman. Because we are designed to cooperate, just like hands, feet, eyelids, and the rows of the upper and lower body.

To act against one another then is contrary to nature; and it is acting against one another to be vexed and to turn away.

Whatever this is that I am, it is a little flesh and breath, and the ruling part.

All that is from the gods is full of Providence. That which is from fortune is not separated from nature or without an interweaving and involution with the things which are ordered by Providence. From thence all things flow; and there is besides necessity, and that which is for the advantage of the whole universe, of which thou art a part.

However, that benefits every aspect of nature that the entirety of nature brings, as well as everything that keeps this nature intact. The cosmos is now preserved both by changes in the constituent materials and by changes in the objects that are made up of those elements. Allow these ideas to suffice for you; allow them to remain unwavering beliefs. However, let go of your desire for literature so that you may pass away joyfully, honestly, and with gratitude to the gods rather than in silence.

Remember how long thou hast been putting off these things, and how often thou hast received an opportunity from the gods, and yet dost not use it. Thou must now at last perceive of what universe thou art a part, and of what administrator of the universe thy existence is an efflux, and that a limit of time is fixed for thee, which if thou dost not use for clearing away the clouds from thy mind, it will go and thou wilt go, and it will never return.

Every moment think steadily as a Roman and a man to do what thou hast in hand with perfect and simple dignity, and feeling of affection, and freedom, and justice; and to give thyself relief from all other thoughts.

Do wrong to thyself, do wrong to thyself, my soul; but thou wilt no longer have the opportunity of honouring thyself. Every man's life is sufficient. But thine is nearly finished, though thy soul reverences not itself but places thy felicity in the souls of others.

Do the things external which fall upon thee distract thee? Give thyself time to learn something new and good, and cease to be whirled around.

But then thou must also avoid being carried about the other way. For those too are triflers who have wearied themselves in life by their activity, and yet have no object to which to direct every movement, and, in a word, all their thoughts.

Therefore they are neither good nor evil. How quickly all things disappear, in the universe the bodies themselves, but in time the remembrance of them; what is the nature of all sensible things, and particularly those which attract with the bait of pleasure or terrify by pain, or are noised abroad by vapoury fame; how worthless, and contemptible, and sordid, and perishable, and dead they are – all this it is the part of the intellectual faculty to observe.

To observe too who these are whose opinions and voices give reputation; what death is, and the fact that, if a man looks at it in itself, and by the abstractive power of reflection resolves into their parts all the things which present themselves to the imagination in it, he will then consider it to be nothing else than an operation of nature; and if anyone is afraid of an operation of nature, he is a child.

This, however, is not only an operation of nature, but it is also a thing which conduces to the purposes of nature. To observe too how man comes near to the deity, and by what part of him, and when this part of man is so disposed.

Nothing is more wretched than a man who traverses everything in a round, and pries into the things beneath the earth, as the poet says, and seeks by conjecture what is in the minds of his neighbours, without perceiving that it is sufficient to attend to the daemon within him, and to reverence it sincerely.

Respect for the daemon also entails keeping it free from passion, carelessness, and discontentment with both gods and humans. Because of their greatness, the objects of the gods deserve to be revered, and objects made by humans should hold a special place in our hearts due to our familial ties.

Occasionally, however, they even evoke sympathy because of people's ignorance of right and wrong—a flaw that is comparable to losing the ability to tell what is white from black.

Though thou shouldst be going to live three thousand years, and as many times ten thousand years, still remember that no man loses any other life than this which he now lives, nor lives any other than this which he now loses. The longest and shortest are thus brought to the same.

For the present is the same to all, though that which perishes is not the same; and so that which is lost appears to be a mere moment. For a man cannot lose either the past or the future: for what a man has not, how can anyone take this from him? These two things then, thou must bear in mind; the one, that all things from eternity are of like forms and come round in a circle, and that it makes no difference whether a man shall see the same things during a hundred years or two hundred, or an infinite time; and the second, that the longest liver and he who will die soonest lose just the same. For the present is the only thing of which a man can be deprived, if it is true that this is the only thing which he has, and that a man cannot lose a thing if he has it not.

Remember that all is opinion. For what was said by the Cynic Monimus is manifest: and manifest too is the use of what was said, if a man receives what may be got out of it as far as it is true.

Book III:

Not only must we take into account that our life is ebbing away every day and that there is a decreasing amount of it left, but we also need to consider the fact that even if a man were to live a longer life, it is unlikely that he would still have the capacity for contemplation that seeks to understand both the divine and human. For if he shall begin to fall into dotage, perspiration and nutrition and imagination and appetite, and whatever else there is of the kind, will not fail; but the power of making use of ourselves, and filling up the measure of our duty, and clearly separating all appearances, and considering whether a man should now depart from life, and whatever else of the kind absolutely requires a disciplined reason, all this is already extinguished. We must make haste then, not only because we are daily nearer to death, but also because the conception of things and the understanding of them cease first.

Hippocrates, after conquering many diseases, yielded to a disease at last. The Chaldeans foretold the fatal hours of multitudes, and fate afterwards carried themselves away. Alexander, Pompey, and Caius Caesar, who so often razed whole cities, and cut off in battle so many myriads of horse and foot, at last departed from this life themselves. Heraclitus, who wrote so much about the conflagration of the universe, died swollen with water, and bedaubed with ox-dung. Vermin destroyed Democritus, the inventor of the philosophy of the atom, and another sort of vermin destroyed Socrates. To what purpose all this? You have gone aboard, made your voyage, arrived to your port, go ashore. If into another life and world, the Gods are also there: if into a state of insensibility; at least you shall be no longer disturbed by sensual pleasure or pain, or be in slavery to this mean corporeal vessel. Is not the soul, which is often enslaved to it, much more excellent than the body? The soul is intelligence and deity. The body, earth, and putrefying blood.

Spend not the remainder of your life in conjectures about others, except where it is subservient to some public interest: conjecturing what such a one is doing, and with what view, what he is saying, what he is thinking, what he is projecting, and such like; this attention to the affairs of others, makes one wander from his own business, the guarding of his own soul.

Book IV

That which rules within, when it is according to nature, is so affected with respect to the events which happen, that it always easily adapts itself to that which is and is presented to it. For it requires no definite material, but it moves towards its purpose, under certain conditions however; and it makes a material for itself out of that which opposes it, as fire lays hold of what falls into it, by which a small light would have been extinguished: but when the fire is strong, it soon appropriates to itself the matter which is heaped on it, and consumes it, and rises higher by means of this very material.

Let no act be done without a purpose, nor otherwise than according to the perfect principles of art.

Men seek retreats for themselves, houses in the country, sea-shores, and mountains; and thou too art wont to desire such things very much. But this is altogether a mark of the most common sort of men, for it is in thy power whenever thou shalt choose to retire into thyself. For nowhere either with more quiet or more freedom from trouble does a man retire than into his own soul, particularly when he has within him such thoughts that by looking into them he is immediately in perfect tranquility; and I affirm that tranquility is nothing else than the good ordering of the mind. Constantly then give to thyself this retreat, and renew thyself; and let thy principles be brief and fundamental, which, as soon as thou shalt recur to them, will be sufficient to cleanse the soul completely, and to send thee back free from all discontent with the things to which thou returnest. For with what art thou discontented? With the badness of men? Recall to thy mind this conclusion, that rational animals exist for one another, and that to endure is a part of justice, and that men do wrong involuntarily; and consider how many already, after mutual enmity, suspicion, hatred, and fighting, have been stretched dead, reduced to ashes; and be quiet at last. But perhaps thou art dissatisfied with that which is assigned to thee out of the universe. Recall to thy recollection this alternative; either there is providence or atoms, fortuitous concurrence of things; or remember the arguments by which it has been proved that the world is a kind of political community, and be quiet at last. But perhaps corporeal things will still fasten upon thee. Consider then further that the mind mingles not with the breath, whether moving gently or violently, when it has once drawn itself apart and discovered its own power, and think also of all that thou hast heard and assented to about pain and pleasure, and be quiet at last. But perhaps the desire of the thing called fame will torment thee. See how soon everything is forgotten, and look at the chaos of infinite time on each side of the present, and the emptiness of applause, and the changeableness and want of judgment in those who pretend to give praise, and the narrowness of the space within which it is circumscribed, and be quiet at last.

Since the entire globe is a point, consider how little a nook this is where you live, how few people live there, and who will honor you. That leaves the following: Remind yourself to withdraw into your small area of your own, and above all, do not divert or overwork yourself; instead, be at ease and view situations from the perspective of a man, a human being, a citizen, and a mortal. However, let there be these two items among those that are ready for your attention. One is that objects do not affect the soul because they are external and unchanging, but our internal opinions are the source of all of our disturbances. The other is that all these things, which thou seest, change immediately and will no longer be; and constantly bear in mind how many of these changes thou hast already witnessed.

The universe is transformation: life is opinion.

If our intellectual part is common, the reason also, in respect of which we are rational beings, is common: if this is so, common also is the reason which commands us what to do, and what not to do; if this is so, there is a common law also; if this is so, we are fellow-citizens; if this is so, we are members of some political community; if this is so, the world is in a manner a state. For of what other common political community will any one say that the whole human race is part of? And from thence, from this common political community comes also our very intellectual faculty and reasoning faculty and our capacity for law; or whence do they come?

For as my earthly part is a portion given to me from certain earth, and that which is watery from another element, and that which is hot and fiery from some peculiar source (for nothing comes out of that which is nothing, as nothing also returns to non-existence), so also the intellectual part comes from some source.

Similar to generation, death is a mystery of nature, consisting of the same elements that are also decomposed into them. It is not something that any man should be ashamed of, as it is consistent with both the rationale of our constitution and the nature of a reasonable animal.

Such people should naturally perform these tasks; it is a matter of necessity. If a man refuses to permit this, he will deny the fig tree its juice. But by all means keep in mind that you and he will both pass away very soon, and before long, not even your names will remain.

Take away thy opinion, and then there is taken away the complaint, "I have been harmed." Take away the complaint, "I have been harmed," and the harm is taken away.

That, which does not make a man worse than he was, also does not make his life worse, nor does it harm him either from without or from within.

The nature of that which is universally useful has been compelled to do this.

Do not have such an opinion of things as he has who does thee wrong, or such as he wishes thee to have, but look at them as they are in truth.

These are the two guidelines that a man should always be prepared to follow: changing one's opinion if someone is nearby who corrects one's perspective or takes one away from one, and only acting upon the reasoning of the governing and legislating faculty as it may apply to men.

However, the only reason for this shift in viewpoint must be a specific persuasive argument, such as what is just or advantageous to everyone, and not merely because it seems nice or improves one's reputation.

Hast thou reason? I have. Why then dost not thou use it? For if this does its own work, what else dost thou wish? Thou hast existed as a part. Thou shalt disappear in that which produced thee; but rather thou shalt be received back into its seminal principle by transmutation.

Many grains of frankincense on the same altar: one falls before, another falls after; but it makes no difference. Within ten days thou wilt seem a god to those to whom thou art now a beast and an ape, if thou wilt return to thy principles and the worship of reason.

How does the air hold souls from eternity if they are everlasting? However, how can the earth hold the remains of people who were buried so long ago? The souls that are removed into the air after existing for a while are transmuted and diffused, and assume a fiery nature by being received into the seminal intelligence of the universe. In this way, they make room for the fresh souls that come to dwell there. Thus, just as the mutation of these bodies after a certain continuance, whatever it may be, and their dissolution make room for other dead bodies.

Book V:

When you find yourself, in a morning, averse to rise, have this thought at hand: I arise to the proper business of a man: And shall I be averse to set about that work for which I was born, and for which I was brought into the universe? Have I this constitution and furniture of soul granted me by nature, that I may lye among bed-cloaths and keep my self warm? But, say you, This state is the pleasanter. Were you then formed for pleasure, and not at all for action, and exercising your powers? Don't you behold the vegetables, the little sparrows, the ants, the spiders, the bees, each of them adorning, on their part, this comely world, as far as their powers can go? And will you decline to act your part as a man for this purpose? Won't you run to that which suits your nature? But, say you, must we not take rest? You must: but nature appoints a measure to it, as it has to eating and drinking.

Judge no speech or action unsuitable to you, which is according to nature; and be not dissuaded from it, by any ensuing censure or reproach of others. But if the speaking or acting thus be honourable, don't undervalue yourself so much as to think you are unworthy to speak or act thus.

These censurers have their own governing parts, and their own inclinations, which you are not to regard, or be diverted by. But go on straight in the way pointed out by your own nature, and the common nature of the whole. They both direct you to the same road.

I walk on in the path which is according to nature, till I fall down to rest, breathing out my last breath into that air I daily drew in, falling into that earth whence my father derived his seed, my mother her blood, my nurse her milk for my nourishment; that earth which supplied me for so many years with meat and drink, and bears me walking on it, and so many ways abusing it.

You cannot readily gain admiration for acuteness: be it so. However, there are numerous other attributes, none of which you can claim you lack by nature. Admire yourself for the things that you can control: your sincerity, gravity, patience, diligence, contempt for pleasure, a heart that never turns away from fate, your contentment with a little, your freedom, your good nature, your temper, your unsolicited talk about superfluities, and your true grandeur of mind. See how many virtues you possess, for which you make no pretense of being naturally incapable? Even so, you willingly fall short of them.

Does any natural defect force you to be querulous at providence? To be tenacious and narrow-hearted? To flatter? To complain of the body, and charge your own faults on it? To fawn on others? To be ostentatious? To be so unsettled in your purposes and projects? No, by the Gods! You might have escaped those vices long ago.

One charge, perhaps, of a slow and tardy understanding, you could not well avoid; but in this, diligence and exercise, might have helped the defect; if you had not neglected it, nor taken a mean pleasure in it.

There are some, who, when they have done you a good office, are apt to charge it to your account, as a great obligation.

We ought to be among those, who, in a manner, seem not to understand what they have done. Well, but ought we not, say you, to understand this point? Is it not the property of the social being, to understand that it acts the social part? Nay, by Jove! To desire too, that its partners and fellows should be sensible it acts thus? What you say is true. Yet if you misapprehend what I said above, you shall remain in one of the former classes, who are led aside from the highest perfection, by some probable specious reasons. But if you desire fully to comprehend what I said, don't be afraid that it will ever retard you in any social action.

This is a prayer of the Athenians, "rain, rain, kind Jupiter! Upon the tilled grounds and pastures of the Athenians." We should either not pray at all, or pray with such simplicity, and such kind affections of free citizens toward our fellows.

As, when 'tis said, that, Aesculapius hath prescribed to one a course of riding, or the cold bath, or walking bare-footed; so it may be said, that the nature presiding in the whole, hath prescribed to one a disease, a maim, a loss of a child, or such like. The word "prescribed," in the former case, imports that he enjoined it as conducing to health; and in the latter too, whatever befalls any one, is appointed as conducive to the purposes of fate or providence. Our very word for happening to one is, to go together appositely, as the squared stones in walls or pyramids are said by the workmen, to fall or join together, and suit each other in a certain position. Now, there is one grand harmonious composition of all things; and as the regular universe is formed such a complete whole of all the particular bodies, so the universal destiny or fate of the whole, is made a complete cause out of all the particular causes. The very vulgar understand what I say. They tell you, "fate ordered this event for such a one, and this was prescribed or appointed for him." Let us understand this even as when we say, "the physician has ordered such things for the patient": for, he prescribes many harsh disagreeable things; which, yet, we embrace willingly, for the sake of health. Conceive, then, the accomplishing and completing the purposes of the universal nature, to be in the universe, what your health is to you, and thus embrace whatever happens, altho' it should appear harsh and disagreeable: because it tends to the health of the universe, to the prosperity and felicity of Jupiter in his administration. He never had permitted this event, had it not conduced to good. We see not any particular nature aiming at or admitting what does not suit the little private system, in which it presides.

19

Should you not on these two accounts embrace and delight in what ever befalls you; one is, that it was formed, and prescribed, and adapted for you, and destined originally by the most venerable causes; the other, that it is subservient to the prosperity, and complete administration of that mind, which governs the whole; nay, by Jupiter! To the stability and permanence of the whole.

For, the whole would be maimed and imperfect, if you broke off any part of this continued connexion, either of parts or causes. Now, you break this off, and destroy it, as far as you can, when you repine at any thing which happens.

What can be easier and sweeter than these things, which are agreeable to nature? Sensual enjoyments by their pleasure ensnare us. But consider: can there be any thing sweeter than magnanimity, liberty, or self-command, simplicity of heart, meekness, purity? What is sweeter than wisdom, when you are conscious of success and security from error in what belongs to the intellectual and scientific powers?

I consist of an active and a material principle. Neither of these shall return to nothing; as they were not made out of nothing. Shall not, then, every part of me be disposed, upon its dissolution, into the correspondent part of the universe; and that, again, be changed into some other part of the universe; and thus to eternity? By such changes I came into being, and my parents too, and their progenitors, from another eternity. We may assert this, though the world be governed by certain grand determined periods of dissolution and renovation.

Reason and the art of the rational agent are powers which are satisfied with themselves and their own proper action, without the aid of what is external or foreign to them. They act from their internal principle, and go straight forward to the end set before them. The actions are called right, or straight, from their straight road to their end.

Nothing can befall any man, which he is not capable by nature to bear.

The like events have befallen others; and they, either through ignorance that the event hath happened, or through ostentation of magnanimity, stand firm and unhurt by them. Strange! Then, that ignorance or ostentation should have more power than wisdom!

The things themselves cannot in the least touch the soul; nor have any access to it; nor can they turn or move it. The soul alone can turn or move itself; and such judgments or opinions, as she condescends to entertain, such she will make all occurrences become to her self.

In one respect, men are the most dearly attached to us, as we are ever obliged to do good to them: but in another respect, as they sometimes obstruct us in our proper offices, they are to be reputed among things indifferent, no less than the sun, the wind, or a savage beast; for, any of these may obstruct us in the discharge of our proper external offices; but, none of them can obstruct our purpose, or our dispositions, because of that reservation and power of turning our course. For the soul can convert and change every impediment of its first intended action, into a more excellent object of action; and thus 'tis for its advantage to be obstructed in action; and it advances in its road, by being stopped in it.

Book VI

Look within. Let neither the peculiar quality of anything nor its value escape thee. All existing things soon change, and they will either be reduced to vapour, if indeed all substance is one, or they will be dispersed. The reason which governs knows what its own disposition is, and what it does, and on what material it works.

The best way of avenging thyself is not to become like the wrong doer. Take pleasure in one thing and rest in it, in passing from one social act to another social act, thinking of God. The ruling principle is that which rouses and turns itself, and while it makes itself such as it is and such as it wills to be, it also makes everything which happens appear to itself to be such as it

wills. In conformity to the nature of the universe every single thing is accomplished, for certainly it is not in conformity to any other nature that each thing is accomplished, either a nature which externally comprehends this, or a nature which is comprehended within this nature, or a nature external and independent of this.

The universe is either a confusion, and a mutual involution of things, and a dispersion; or it is unity and order and providence. If then it is the former, why do I desire to tarry in a fortuitous combination of things and such a disorder? And why do I care about anything else than how I shall at last become earth?

And why am I disturbed, for the dispersion of my elements will happen whatever I do. But if the other supposition is true, I venerate, and I am firm, and I trust in him who governs.

When thou hast been compelled by circumstances to be disturbed in a manner, quickly return to thyself and do not continue out of tune longer than the compulsion lasts; for thou wilt have more mastery over the harmony by continually recurring to it.

If thou hadst a step-mother and a mother at the same time, thou wouldst be dutiful to thy step-mother, but still thou wouldst constantly return to thy mother. Let the court and philosophy now be to thee step-mother and mother: return to philosophy frequently and repose in her, through whom what thou meetest with in the court appears to thee tolerable, and thou appearest tolerable in the court.

When we have meat before us and such eatables we receive the impression, that this is the dead body of a fish, and this is the dead body of a bird or of a pig; and again, that this Falernian is only a little grape juice, and this purple robe some sheep's wool dyed with the blood of a shell-fish: such then are these impressions, and they reach the things themselves and penetrate them, and so we see what kind of things they are.

Most of the things which the multitude admire are referred to objects of the most general kind, those which are held together by cohesion or natural organization, such as stones, wood, fig-trees, vines, olives. But those which are admired by men who are a little more reasonable are referred to the things which are held together by a living principle, as flocks, herds.

Things kept together by a rational soul are admired by more educated persons. This rational soul need not be global; it can be rational insofar as it is a soul competent in a particular art or other field, or it can be reasonable insofar as it has many slaves. However, this is the only thing that matters to someone who values a rational soul—a soul that is universal and suited for political life. Above all, he maintains his soul in a state and activity that are consistent with reason and social life, and he works in tandem with like-minded people to achieve this goal.

Some things are hurrying into existence, and others are hurrying out of it; and of that which is coming into existence part is already extinguished. Motions and changes are continually renewing the world, just as the uninterrupted course of time is always renewing the infinite duration of ages. In this flowing stream then, on which there is no abiding, what is there of the things which hurry by on which a man would set a high price? It would be just as if a man should fall in love with one of the sparrows which fly by, but it has already passed out of sight. Something of this kind is the very life of every man, like the exhalation of the blood and the respiration of the air. For such as it is to have once drawn in the air and to have given it back, which we do every moment, just the same is it with the whole respiratory power, which thou didst receive at thy birth yesterday and the day before, to give it back to the element from which thou didst first draw it.

Neither is transpiration, as in plants, a thing to be valued, nor respiration, as in domesticated animals and wild beasts, nor the receiving of impressions by the appearances of things, nor being moved by desires as puppets by strings, nor assembling in herds, nor being nourished by food; for this is just like the act of separating and parting with the useless part of our food. What then is worth being valued? To be received with clapping of hands? No. Neither must we value the clapping of tongues, for the praise which comes from the many is a clapping of tongues. Suppose then that thou hast given up this worthless thing called fame, what remains that is worth valuing?

This, in my opinion, is the goal that all occupations and artistic endeavors lead to: moving yourself and exercising self-control in accordance with your right constitution. Because this is the ultimate goal of all art, everything created should be tailored to the purpose for which it was intended. This is the goal shared by the horse-breaker, the person who trains dogs, and the person who plants vines. However, youth education and instruction have a purpose. Herein lies the significance of education and instruction.

Book VII

Explores themes of mortality, divinity, and the importance of honesty and self-improvement.

What is vice? 'Tis what you have often seen. Have this thought ready on all emergences that they are such things as you have often seen: you'll find all things, earlier or later, just the same. Such matters as fill all histories of the ancient, or middle, or present ages: of such things, all cities and families are full. Nothing is new. Every thing is ordinary, and of short duration.

How can the great life lessons ever die in the soul unless the beliefs that support them are suppressed? Furthermore, you still have the ability to rekindle and revitalize these sincere beliefs. I can always feel the way I should about these kinds of things, so why am I bothered? My soul doesn't care about what is outside of it. Be so convinced that you stand erect and resolute. You can resurrect whenever you'd like. Think over things once more, just as you have in the past. This is coming back to life.

The conceited carelessness regarding performances, scenic depictions, herds and flocks, fighting, small bones thrown into a pond to settle disputes between small dogs, baits thrown into a fish pond, the laboring of Ants and their carrying of loads, the flapping of scared flies, the uncontrollably agitated puppets by wires! We should continue in the face of such things amicably, without becoming angry with them, and accept that each individual is valuable in the same way as the things he desires are valuable.

In Conversation, we should give good heed to what is said; and in business, to what is done: in the former, that we may understand what is signified; and, in the latter, to what end it is referred.

Is my understanding sufficient for this subject or not? If it is sufficient, I use it as an Instrument given me by the universal nature for this work: If it is not, I either give place in this work to those who can better execute it; unless it be some way incumbent as duty upon me; and, in that case, I execute it as well as I can, taking the aid of those, who, by directing my mind, can accomplish something seasonable and useful to the public. For whatever I do, whether by myself, or with the assistance of others, ought to be directed to that, alone, which is useful and suitable to the public.

How many people who were formerly highly acclaimed are now consigned to obscurity? And how many people who once sang others' praises are now completely gone?

Accepting help is nothing to be ashamed about. Your goal should be to carry out your responsibilities, just as a soldier would rush a wall breach. What if you are unable to mount the works by yourself due to your lameness? You can do it with other people's help.

Don't worry about the future; you will encounter occurrences with the same rationale that you already use in your current concerns.

All things are linked with each other, and bound together with a sacred bond: Scarce is there one thing quite foreign to another. They are all arranged together in their proper places, and jointly adorn the same world. There is one orderly graceful disposition of the whole. There is one God in the whole. There is one substance, one law, and one reason common to all intelligent beings, and one truth; as there must be one sort of perfection to all beings, who are of the same nature, and partake of the same rational power.

Every thing material shall soon vanish, and be swallowed up in the matter of the whole. Every active principle shall soon be resumed into the intelligence and cause of the whole. And the memory of every thing shall soon be buried in eternity.

In the rational being, the same conduct is agreeable to nature, and agreeable to reason.

Either show yourself as one always upright, or as one well corrected and amended.

Despite their geographical distance, all rational creatures are part of an organized body since they are both suited for a single cooperative function. If you tell yourself, "I am a part of that great rational body or system," on a regular basis, this concept will have a greater impact on your heart. Merely identifying as a member of humanity does not imply that you truly love people, nor does doing something deserving of praise in the short term satisfy you in the long run. You only act morally out of responsibility and obligation, not in an effort to benefit oneself to the fullest extent possible.

Let external things affect, as they please, the things which can be affected by them; let those complain of them which suffer by them. But if I can prevent any apprehension that the event is evil, I am not hurt. And it is in my power to prevent it.

Let any one do or say what he pleases, I must be a good man. Just as if the gold, the emerald, or the purple were always saying, let men do or say what they please, I must continue an emerald, and retain my luster.

Is not the governing part the sole cause of its own disturbance? Does it not raise in itself its fears, its sorrows, its desires? If any other thing can raise its fears or sorrows, let it do so. 'Tis in its own power not to be moved by opinions about such incidents.

Let the despicable body take thought, if it can, for itself; lest it suffer any thing, and complain when it suffers. The soul which is terrified or dejected, or which is struck with imaginations or opinions about such things, would suffer nothing, if you would not give it up to such imaginations. The governing part is free from all indigence or dependence, if it doesn't make itself indigent. In like manner, it may be free from all disturbance and obstruction, if it don't disturb and obstruct itself.

To have good-fortune is to have a good divinity governing our lot; or a good divinity, within, governing us. Be gone, then, imagination! Go, by the Gods! As you came: for I have no more use for you. You came, according to the old custom: I am not angry with you; only, be gone.

Does one dread a change? What can arise without changes? What is more acceptable or more usual to the nature of the whole? Can you warm your bagnio, unless wood undergoes a change? Can you be nourished, unless your food is changed? Or, can anything useful be accomplished, without changes? Don't you see, then, that your undergoing a change, too, may be equally necessary to the nature of the whole?

All distinct bodies, all of the same kind, run through the material of the universe like a torrent and cooperate with the whole as do the same parts of our own body. How many Epictetus, Socrates, and Chrysippus have been absorbed by time? Allow this idea to cross your mind regarding every individual and situation.

Just with regard to this, I am careful to ensure that I don't do anything that would be contrary to a man's nature, that I follow the proper procedure, or that I do it at the wrong moment.

The time approaches when you shall forget all things, and be forgotten by all.

'Tis the part of a man to love even those who offend him; and this one may do, if he would consider that those who offend are our kindred by nature; that they offend through ignorance, and unwillingly; and that, in a little, both we and they must die: and especially, that they have done thee no damage; for, they cannot make thy soul worse than it was before.

The ruling nature originates from the universal substance, much like a colt does from wax. It then changes that again, forming a tree from its matter, a man from it, and something else from it, all of which existed for a short while. As there was nothing gloomy about a chest's initial joining together, there can be nothing gloomy about it being pulled apart.

A wrathful countenance is exceedingly against nature. When the countenance is often thus deformed, its beauty dies, and cannot be revived again. By this very thing you may apprehend that it is against reason. If the sense of moral evil is gone, what reason could one have for desiring to live?

All things you behold, shall the nature presiding in the universe change; and out of their substance make other things; and others, again, out of theirs; that the universe may be always new.

When one has offended, or done anything wrong; consider what opinion of his, about some good, or evil, hath led him into this misconduct. When you discover this, you will pity him; and neither be surprised, nor angry. Perhaps, you yourself may imagine the same thing, or some such like thing, to be good. If you don't at all look upon such things as good or evil, you can easily be indulgent and gentle to those who are in a mistake.

Don't let your thoughts dwell upon what you want, so much, as, upon what you have. And consider the things you enjoy, which are dearest to you; how earnestly and anxiously you would desire them, if you wanted them: And yet be on your guard; lest, by your delighting in the enjoyment of such things, you endure yourself to value them too much; so that if you should lose them, you would be much disturbed.

Wind yourself up inside of yourself. The natural ability of the rational ruling portion is to fully fulfill itself by acting justly and finding peace in the process.

Remove all imaginings. Put an end to the passions' ruthless urges. Trace the current moment and understand the nature of everything that occurs, whether it be to you or to others. Differentiate between the active principle and the substance. Think carefully on the past hour. Let the guilt lie where it belongs—where someone else's fault is committed.

Book VIII

This reflection also tends to the removal of the desire of empty fame, that it is no longer in thy power to have lived the whole of thy life, or at least thy life from thy youth upwards, like a philosopher; but both to many others and to thyself it is plain that thou art far from philosophy.

Thou hast fallen into disorder then, so that it is no longer easy for thee to get the reputation of a philosopher; and thy plan of life also opposes it. If you have indeed seen the true nature of the issue, set aside any concerns about how you will appear to others and accept that you will spend the remainder of your life doing what your nature dictates. Once you have experienced many wanderings without finding contentment anywhere— not in syllogisms, fortune, renown, delight, or anywhere else—observe what it wills and let nothing else divert you. So where is it? In carrying out what the nature of man demands.

How then shall a man do this? If he has principles from which come his affects and his acts. What principles? Those which relate to good and bad: the belief that there is nothing good for man, which does not make him just, temperate, manly, free; and that there is nothing bad, which does not do the contrary to what has been mentioned.

On the occasion of every act ask thyself, How is this with respect to me? Shall I repent of it? A little time and I am dead, and all is gone. What more do I seek, if what I am now doing is work of an intelligent living being, and a social being, and one who is under the same law with

God? Alexander and Gaius and Pompeius, what are they in comparison with Diogenes and Heraclitus and Socrates? For they were acquainted with things, and their causes (forms), and their matter, and the ruling principles of these men were the same. But as to the others, how many things had they to care for, and to how many things were they slaves? Consider that men will do the same things nevertheless, even though thou shouldst burst.

The most important thing is to remember that everything happens according to the global law, so don't worry. Soon, you will disappear completely, just like Hadrian and Augustus did. Next, with your eyes fixed steadily on your work, examine it while keeping in mind that it is your responsibility to be a good man and that this is what man's nature requires. Do this without deviating from it, and speak whatever comes to mind as the most just, as long as you do it with humility, kindness, and honesty.

The nature of the universal has this work to do, to remove to that place the things which are in this, to change them, to take them away hence, and to carry them there. All things are change, yet we need not fear anything new. All things are familiar to us; but the distribution of them still remains the same.

Thou hast not leisure or ability to read. But thou hast leisure or ability to check arrogance: thou hast leisure to be superior to pleasure and pain: thou hast leisure to be superior to love of fame, and not to be vexed at stupid and ungrateful people, nay even to care for them.

Let no man any longer hear thee finding fault with the court life or with thy own.

Repentance is a kind of self-reproof for having neglected something useful; but that which is good must be something useful, and the perfect good man should look after it. But no such man would ever repent of having refused any sensual pleasure. Pleasure then is neither good nor useful.

Whatever man thou meetest with, immediately say to thyself: What opinions has this man about good and bad? For if with respect to pleasure and pain and the causes of each, and with respect to fame and ignominy, death and life, he has such and such opinions, it will seem nothing wonderful or strange to me, if he does such and such things; and I shall bear in mind that he is compelled to do so. Remember that as it is a shame to be surprised if the fig-tree produces figs, so it is to be surprised if the world produces such and such things of which it is productive; and for the physician and the helmsman it is a shame to be surprised, if a man has a fever, or if the wind is unfavourable.

Remember that to change thy opinion and to follow him who corrects thy error is as consistent with freedom as it is to persist in thy error.

For it is thy own, the activity which is exerted according to thy own movement and judgement, and indeed according to thy own understanding too.

If a thing is in thy own power, why dost thou do it? But if it is in the power of another, whom dost thou blame? The atoms (chance) or the gods? Both are foolish. Thou must blame nobody. For if thou canst, correct that which is the cause; but if thou canst not do this, correct at least the thing itself; but if thou canst not do even this, of what use is it to thee to find fault? For nothing should be done without a purpose.

What good is it then for the ball to be thrown up, or harm for it to come down, or even to have fallen? And what good is it to the bubble while it holds together, or what harm when it is burst? The same may be said of a light also. Turn it (the body) inside out, and see what kind of thing it is; and when it has grown old, what kind of thing it becomes, and when it is diseased.

Both the one who praises and the one who is praised, as well as the rememberer and the remembered, have a short lifespan; this is only in one small corner of the world, and nobody agrees with themselves here either. The entire planet is also a point. Pay attention to the issue at hand, regardless of whether it involves a word, an act, or an opinion. You bear this with justification, as you would sooner become good tomorrow than be good today.

Am I doing anything? I do it with reference to the good of mankind. Does anything happen to me? I receive it and refer it to the gods, and the source of all things, from which all that happens is

derived. Such as bathing appears to thee- oil, sweat, dirt, filthy water, all things disgusting- so is every part of life and everything.

Lucilla saw Verus die, and then Lucilla died. Secunda saw Maximusdie, and then Secunda died. Epitynchanus saw Diotimus die, and Epitynchanus died. Antoninus saw Faustina die, and then Antoninus died. Such is everything.

It is satisfaction to a man to do the proper works of a man. Now it is a proper work of a man to be benevolent to his own kind, to despise the movements of the senses, to form a just judgement of plausible appearances, and to take a survey of the nature of the universe and of the things which happen in it.

You have three relationships with other things: one with your surrounding body, one with the divine cause from whom everything originates, and a third with those you coexist with.

Pain is either an evil to the body—let the body express its opinions on the matter—or to the spirit; yet, the soul has the ability to preserve its own peace and tranquility and resist the notion that pain is bad. Since all judgments, actions, desires, and aversions originate from inside, no evil can rise to such a height.

Wipe out thy imaginations by often saying to thyself: now it is in my power to let no badness be in this soul, nor desire nor any perturbation at all; but looking at all things I see what is their nature, and I use each according to its value.

Remember this power which thou hast from nature. Speak both in the senate and to every man, whoever he may be, appropriately, not with any affectation: use plain discourse. Augustus' court, wife, daughter, descendants, ancestors, sister, Agrippa, kinsmen, intimates, friends, Areius, Maecenas, physicians and sacrificing priests- the whole court is dead. Then turn to the rest, not considering the death of a single man, but of a whole race, as of the Pompeii; and that which is inscribed on the tombs- The last of his race. Then consider what trouble those before them have had that they might leave a successor; and then, that of necessity some one must be the last. Again here consider the death of a whole race.

It is thy duty to order thy life well in every single act; and if every act does its duty, as far as is possible, be content; and no one is able to hinder thee so that each act shall not do its duty.- But something external will stand in the way.- Nothing will stand in the way of thy acting justly and soberly and considerately.- But perhaps some other active power will be hindered.- Well, but by acquiescing in the hindrance and by being content to transfer thy efforts to that which is allowed, another opportunity of action is immediately put before thee in place of that which was hindered, and one which will adapt itself to this ordering of which we are speaking.

Receive wealth or prosperity without arrogance; and be ready to let it go.

If thou didst ever see a hand cut off, or a foot, or a head, lying anywhere apart from the rest of the body, such does a man make himself, as far as he can, who is not content with what happens, and separates himself from others, or does anything unsocial.

Book IX

He who does an injury is guilty of impiety. For, since the nature of the whole has formed the rational animals for one another; each for being useful to the other according to his merit, and never hurtful; he who transgresses this her will, is thus guilty of impiety against the most ancient and venerable of the Gods. Since everything that exists has a nature similar to its causes, everything that exists has the same nature as the whole. She is sometimes referred to as truth and is the source of all truths. Therefore, a person who lies knowingly commits impiety inasmuch as he does harm by lying; likewise, a person who lies unintentionally commits impiety inasmuch as his speech contradicts the essence of the whole and he behaves dishonorably by going against the orderly structure of the universe. Since nature had provided him with the ability to discriminate between truth and untruth, he is now unable to do so since he is fighting against its nature and design.

When I state that common nature views them as indifferent, I mean that she views their occurrence or non-occurrence as indifferent events in the grand established series, in which things exist and follow upon others, suitably to that providence and design which, at a certain period, set about this fair structure and arrangement of the universe; after she had conceived and fixed the plan of all that was to exist; and appointed the distinct powers which were to produce the several substances, changes, and successions.

It were the more desirable lot, to depart from among men, unacquainted with falsehood, hypocrisy, luxury, or vanity. The next choice were to expire, when cloyed with these vices, rather than continue among them: and does not even experience, yet, persuade you to fly from amidst the plague? For a corruption of the intellectual part is far more a plague than any pestilential distemper and change of this surrounding fluid which we breathe. The one is only a pestilence to animals, as they are animals; but the other to men, as they are men.

Don't despise death; but receive it well-pleased; as it is one of the things which nature wills. For such as it is to be young, to be old, to grow up, to be full grown; to breed teeth, and beard, and grow grey; to beget, to go with child, to be delivered; and undergo the other natural effects which the seasons of your life produce; such is it also to be dissolved. It becomes a man of wisdom neither to be inconsiderate, impetuous, or ostentatiously contemptuous about death; but await the season of it, as of one of the operations of nature. As you are now awaiting the season when the fetus shall come out of the womb of your wife, thus await the season when your soul shall fall out of these its teguments.

Here's a popular support that speaks to the heart if you also want it: you will have an extremely easy time accepting death if you think about the things you are leaving behind and the manners of the confused crowd you are leaving behind. At the same time, though, you shouldn't take offense at them; in fact, you should treat them with kindness and bear with them gently.

However, keep in mind that you are not being removed from guys who share your beliefs because if that were the case, that alone may cause you to regress and be imprisoned in life. Instead, you would be placed among men who share your values and aspirations.

He who does wrong, does a wrong to himself. He who is injurious, does evil to himself, by making himself evil.

Men are often unjust by omissions, as well as by actions.

Be satisfied with your present sentiments of things, if certain; your present course of action, if social; and, your present temper of mind, if well-pleased with every thing which comes from the universal cause.

Wipe out the fancies of imagination: stop all eager impulses to action: extinguish keen desires; and keep the governing part master of itself.

Among the irrationals one animal-soul is distributed; the rational, again, partake of one intellectual soul: just as there is one earth to all things earthy; and as all of us, who are induced with sight, and animated, see with one light and breathe one air.

Anything that shares a characteristic with another has a strong inclination to be similar to it. The aqueous and earthy elements naturally flow together, as does the aerial element; therefore, intercepting partitions and violence are required to prevent their confluence. Because of the elementary fire, everything that has the potential to catch fire wants to gravitate higher. This means that even relatively dry materials can catch fire quickly because there isn't as much of anything to prevent it from starting.

Thus, now, also, whatever partakes of the common intellectual nature, hastens, in like manner, or rather more, to mingle with, and adhere to what is a-kin to it. For the more it excels other natures, the stronger is its tendency to mix with and adhere to what is a-kin to it. Thus, among irrational animals, we easily observe swarms, and herds, nurture of their young, and, as it were, mutual loves: for they have animal-souls; and the mutual attraction is found stronger in the more noble nature; such as was not found in plants, nor in stones, or wood. And then among the rational animals, begun civil-societies, friendships, families, and assemblies; nay, treaties, and truces, even in war.

Among beings, again, still more excellent, there subsists, tho' they are placed far asunder, a certain kind of union: as among the stars. So can that higher excellence cause these so very different beings to sympathize with each other.

But take attention of what happens [between us:] Since only thinkers appear to have overlooked civic duty and a common goal of unification! Not just in this place is the social convergence visible! The thing engulfs and imprisons them even after they take off. since nature always prevails. You'll see what I mean if you listen carefully. A man who is cut off and alone from everyone else can be found connecting to nothing earthly more quickly than an earthly object.

Man, God, and the universe, all bear fruit; and each in their own seasons. Custom indeed has appropriated the expression to the vine, and the like; but that is nothing. Reason has its fruit too, both social and private. And it produces just such other things as reason itself is.

If you can, teach them better. If not, remember that the virtue of meekness was given you to be exercised on such occasions. Nay, the Gods also exercise meekness and patience toward them; and even aid them in their pursuits of some things; as of health, wealth, glory. So gracious are they! You may be so too. Or, say, who hinders you?

Bear toil and pain, not as if wretched under it; nor as wanting to be pitied, or admired. But will only one thing; always to act, or refrain, as social wisdom requires.

Today I have escaped from every dangerous accident: or, rather, I have thrown out from me every dangerous accident. For they were not without; but within, in my own opinions.

All these things are, in our experience of them, customary; in their continuance, but for a day; and, in their matter, sordid. All at present, such as they were in the times of those we have buried.

The things themselves stand with out-doors, by themselves; and neither know, nor declare to us any thing concerning themselves. What declares, then, and pronounces, concerning them? The governing part.

The good and evil of the rational animal created for society are found in action rather than in passive feeling, just as its virtues and vices are found in action rather than in passive feeling.

It is neither wicked nor beneficial for the stone to fall or to have risen up.

See what sort of judges you dread and what kind of judges they are about themselves when you go into their governing sector.

Everything is always changing, including you. You are constantly changing and becoming more corrupt in certain ways, just like the rest of the universe.

The fault of another you must leave with himself.

The cessation of any action, the extinction of any keen desire, or of any opinion, is as it were a death to them. This is no evil. Turn, now to your different ages; such as childhood, youth, manhood, old-age; for every change of these is a death. Is there any thing alarming here? Go, now, to your life; first as it was under your grand-father, then as it was under your mother; and then as it was under your father: and, as you find there many other alterations, changes, and endings, ask yourself, was there any thing in these to alarm me? Thus, neither is there, in the ending, ceasing, and change, of your whole life.

Have speedy recourse to your own governing part, and to that of the whole, and to that of this man [who has offended you.] To your own, that you may make it a mind disposed to justice: to that of the whole, that you may remember of what you are a part: and to that of this man, that you may know whether he has acted out of ignorance, or design; and that you may, at the same time, consider, he is your kinsman.

A torrent is the source of the entire thing. It carries with it everything. And how worthless are those miserable animals who think they know something about state issues, and think they can combine the wisdom of the politician and the philosopher within themselves! Just foam! Do you, O man, whatever it is that nature wants of you? If you are able, go about it. Don't look around to see if anyone is paying attention, and don't hold out hope for Plato's commonwealth. However, view the incidence of this particular item as no minor issue, and be satisfied even if it has the slightest success.

For who can change the opinions of those men? Now, without a change of their opinions, what is it else but a slavery they are groaning under, while they pretend a willing obedience? Come, now, and tell me of Alexander, Phillip, and Demetrius Phalereus. They know best whether they understood what the common nature requir'd of them; and train'd themselves accordingly. But, if they designed only an outward shew, to gain the applause and admiration of men, no-body has condemned me to imitate them. The business of philosophy is simple, meek, and modest. Don't lead me away after [the smoke and vapour of] a vain glorious stateliness.

Contemplate, as from some height, the innumerable herds; and innumerable religious rites, and navigation of all kinds, in storms, and calms; the different states of those who are coming into life, those who are associating in life, those who are leaving life. Consider also the life which others have lived formerly; the life they will live after you, and the life the barbarous nations now live: And how many know not even your name; how many will quickly forget it; how many, who perhaps praise you now, will quickly blame you: And, that neither a surviving fame is a thing of value; nor present glory; nor any thing at all [of that kind.]

Tranquility as to what happens by external causes: Justice in what proceeds from the active principle within you: that is, a bent of will and course of action which rests and is satisfied in its having been exerted for the good of society; as being suited to your nature.

By removing a great deal of unnecessary items that clog your mind and cause you discomfort, you can create a lot more space and tranquility for yourself. As, for example, by understanding, by your judgment, the entire universe; by thinking about the era you live in; and by thinking about the rapid changes that occur in every thing, specifically how short the time it takes for something to arise and dissolve; how vast the space of time that exists before something arises and how equally infinite the time that remains after something dissolves.

All things you see will quickly perish; and those, who behold them perishing, will themselves also quickly perish: and he who died in extreme old-age, will be in the same condition with him who died early.

What kind of governing parts have these men! And about what things are they earnestly employed! And on what accounts do they love and honor! Imagine their minds naked before you. When they fancy their censures hurt, or their praises, profit us; how great their self-conceit!

Loss is nothing else but change: and in this delights the nature of the whole; by which all things are formed well. From the beginning of ages they have been managed in the same way: and to all eternity, such like things will be. How can you say both that all things were formed, and that all shall be always, in a bad state? Among so many Gods, it seems, there is no sufficient power found out to rectify those things. But the universe is condemned to remain involved in never-ceasing evils.

How putrid the material substance of every thing! Water, dust, little bones, and nauseous excretions. Again; marble is but the concreted humors of the earth; gold and silver its heavy dregs: Our clothes but hairs; and the purple color of them, blood. All other things are of the same kind. The animal spirit too is another such thing, passing always from one change to another.

Enough of this wretched life, of repining, and apish trifling. Why are you disturbed? Are any of these things new? What astonishes you? Is it the active principle? View it well. Or, is it the material? View it also well. Besides these there is nothing else. Nay, I obtest you by the Gods, come at length to more simplicity of heart, and equity in your sentiments. It is the same thing whether you have observed these things for a hundred years, or for three.

If he is at fault, then the blame lies with him; conversely, it's possible that he is innocent. Either way, everything that happens in the entire originates from a single intelligent source, and as such, no portion of the whole should be complaining about what happens to it. Or everything is made of atoms, with nothing more than a dissipation and a disarray of pieces. Then, why are you upset? You can still keep [your ruling portion] free from chance, but you may tell it you're dead, rotting, lying, joining the herd, being fed, and becoming a barbarian.

Either the Gods have no power at all [to aid men in anything;] or they have power. If, then, they have no power, why do you pray? But if they have power, why don't you chuse to pray to them to enable you, neither to fear any of these things, [which are not in our own power] nor desire any of them, nor be grieved about any of them; rather than for the having them, or the not having them. For, most certainly, if they can aid men at all, they can also aid them in this.

You can counter that I have the authority because the gods have given me this. So, is it not preferable to make use of the resources at your disposal and maintain your freedom rather than worrying endlessly about resources beyond your control and turning into a helpless slave? Furthermore, who said the gods don't support us in the areas where we are capable of helping ourselves? So start praying for these things, and you will see.

One prays; how shall I enjoy this woman! Do you; how shall I have no desire to enjoy her! Another; how shall I be freed from this man! Do you; how shall I not need to be freed from him! A third; how shall I prevent the loss of my child! Do you; how shall I not be afraid to lose him! Upon the whole; turn your prayers this way, and look what will be the effect.

Epicurus says: "When I was sick, my conversations were not about the diseases of this poor body: nor did I speak of any such things to those who came to me. But continued to discourse of these principles of natural philosophy, I had before established: And was chiefly intent on this; how the intellectual part, tho' it partakes of such violent commotions of the body, might remain undisturbed, and preserve its own proper good. Nor did I allow the physicians to make a noise, and vaunt, as if doing something of great moment. But my life continued pleasant and happy."

What he did, when under a disease, do you, also, if you fall into one, or are under any other uneasy circumstances: that is, never depart from your philosophy, whatever befalls you; nor run into the silly way of the vulgar, and such as are unacquainted with nature. It is the common maxim of all sects of philosophy; to be wholly intent on what they are doing, and the instrument or means by which they do it.

Book X

Wilt thou, then, my soul, never be good and simple and one and naked, more manifest than the body which surrounds thee? Wilt thou never enjoy an affectionate and contented disposition? Wilt thou never be full and without a want of any kind, longing for nothing more, nor desiring anything, either animate or inanimate, for the enjoyment of pleasures? Nor yet desiring time wherein thou shalt have longer enjoyment, or place, or pleasant climate, or society of men with whom thou mayest live in harmony?

Will you, however, be content with your current situation and everything that surrounds you? Will you persuade yourself that everything is yours and that it is a gift from the gods? Will you conclude that everything is well and that everything will work out for you? Will they provide for the preservation of the ideal human being—the good, just, and beautiful—that creates and holds everything and encompasses everything that is dissolved to make room for more of the same?

Wilt thou never be such that thou shalt so dwell in community with gods and men as neither to find fault with them at all, nor to be condemned by them?

If your nature, as far as you are a living person, will not be worsened by it, then observe what thy nature requires, to the extent that thou art guided by nature alone. Then, do it and accept it. The next thing you have to do is pay attention to what your nature demands of you as a living being. And you may allow yourself to do all of this as long as it doesn't worsen your nature—that is, if you're a reasonable animal. However, this also means that the rational animal is a political (social) animal. So follow these guidelines and don't worry about anything else.

Everything which happens either happens in such wise as thou art formed by nature to bear it, or as thou art not formed by nature to bear it. If, then, it happens to thee in such way as thou art formed by nature to bear it, do not complain, but bear it as thou art formed by nature to bear it.

But if it happens in such wise as thou art not formed by nature to bear it, do not complain, for it will perish after it has consumed thee.

Remember, however, that thou art formed by nature to bear everything, with respect to which it depends on thy own opinion to make it endurable and tolerable, by thinking that it is either thy interest or thy duty to do this. If a man is mistaken, instruct him kindly and show him his error. But if thou art not able, blame thyself, or blame not even thyself. Whatever may happen to thee, it was prepared for thee from all eternity; and the implication of causes was from eternity spinning the thread of thy being, and of that which is incident to it.

Whether the universe is a concourse of atoms, or nature is a system, let this first be established, that I am a part of the whole which is governed by nature; next, I am in a manner intimately related to the parts which are of the same kind with myself. For remembering this, inasmuch as I am a part, I shall be discontented with none of the things which are assigned to me out of the whole; for nothing is injurious to the part, if it is for the advantage of the whole. For the whole contains nothing which is not for its advantage; and all natures indeed have this common principle, but the nature of the universe has this principle besides, that it cannot be compelled even by any external cause to generate anything harmful to itself. By remembering, then, that I am a part of such a whole, I shall be content with everything that happens. And inasmuch as I am in a manner intimately related to the parts which are of the same kind with myself, I shall do nothing unsocial, but I shall rather direct myself to the things which are of the same kind with myself, and I shall turn an my efforts to the common interest, and divert them from the contrary. Now, if these things are done so, life must flow on happily, just as thou mayest observe that the life of a citizen is happy, who continues a course of action which is advantageous to his fellow-citizens, and is content with whatever the state may assign to him.

The elements that comprise the entirety—that is, everything that is naturally understood in the universe—shall inevitably die; yet, this should be interpreted to mean that they must transform. However, if this is inherently both a bad thing and a need for the parts, the whole would not last in a state of excellent health, as the parts are malleable and made to die in different ways. For did nature intend for the things that are a part of her to be bad, to be vulnerable to evil, and to inevitably descend into evil, or did these outcomes occur naturally without her knowledge? Indeed, these two hypotheses are astounding.

When thou hast assumed these names, good, modest, true, rational, a man of equanimity, and magnanimous, take care that thou dost not change these names; and if thou shouldst lose them, quickly return to them.

And remember that the term Rational was intended to signify a discriminating attention to every several thing and freedom from negligence; and that Equanimity is the voluntary acceptance of the things which are assigned to thee by the common nature; and that Magnanimity is the elevation of the intelligent part above the pleasurable or painful sensations of the flesh, and above that poor thing called fame, and death, and all such things.

If, therefore, you continue to identify with these identities without wanting to be addressed by them by others, you will cease to be yourself and begin a new existence. Because to stay as you have been and to be torn apart and defiled in this way is the mark of a very foolish man who is overly fond of his life.

It's similar to those half-devoured fighters with wild beasts who, despite their gore and wounds, still want to be kept alive for the next day even though they will be subjected to the same bites and claws.

Therefore fix thyself in the possession of these few names: and if thou art able to abide in them, abide as if thou wast removed to certain islands of the Happy. But if thou shalt perceive that thou fallest out of them and dost not maintain thy hold, go courageously into some nook where thou shalt maintain them, or even depart at once from life, not in passion, but with simplicity and freedom and modesty, after doing this one laudable thing at least in thy life, to have gone out of it thus. In order, however, to the remembrance of these names, it will greatly help thee, if thou rememberest the gods, and that they wish not to be flattered, but wish all reasonable beings to be made like themselves; and if thou rememberest that what does the work of a fig-tree is a fig-tree, and that what does the work of a dog is a dog, and that what does the work of a bee is a bee, and that what does the work of a man is a man. Mimi, war, astonishment, torpor, slavery, will daily wipe out those holy principles of thine. How many things without studying nature dost thou imagine, and how many dost thou neglect?

But it is thy duty so to look on and so to do everything, that at the same time the power of dealing with circumstances is perfected, and the contemplative faculty is exercised, and the confidence which comes from the knowledge of each several thing is maintained without showing it, but yet not concealed. For when wilt thou enjoy simplicity, when gravity, and when the knowledge of every several thing, both what it is in substance, and what place it has in the universe, and how long it is formed to exist and of what things it is compounded, and to whom it can belong, and who are able both to give it and take it away?

A spider feels proud of itself when it catches a fly, another when it catches a helpless hare, still another when it catches a small fish in a net, still another when it catches wild boars, still another when it catches bears, and still another when it catches Sarmatians. If thou lookst at these robbers' ideas, are they not?

Develop a thoughtful perspective on how everything transforms into itself. Pay close attention to this perspective at all times. Practice this aspect of philosophy. Nothing is more suited to elicit generosity than this.

Such a man has put off the body, and as he sees that he must, no one knows how soon, go away from among men and leave everything here, he gives himself up entirely to just doing in all his actions, and in everything else that happens he resigns himself to the universal nature. But as to what any man shall say or think about him or do against him, he never even thinks of it, being himself contented with these two things, with acting justly in what he now does, and being satisfied with what is now assigned to him; and he lays aside all distracting and busy pursuits, and desires nothing else than to accomplish the straight course through the law, and by accomplishing the straight course to follow God.

You have the ability to determine what has to be done, so why should you be suspicious? If you see clearly, proceed down this path with satisfaction and don't turn back. If not, halt and consult the most knowledgeable advisors. If there are other factors that resist you, proceed with caution and according to your abilities, adhering to what seems right.

Because achieving this goal is ideal, let your failure stem from trying to do it. A person who always acts rationally is at once calm and proactive, as well as happy and composed.

Inquire of thyself as soon as thou wakest from sleep, whether it will make any difference to thee, if another does what is just and right. It will make no difference. Thou hast not forgotten, I suppose, that those who assume arrogant airs in bestowing their praise or blame on others, are such as they are at bed and at board, and thou hast not forgotten what they do, and what they avoid and what they pursue, and how they steal and how they rob, not with hands and feet, but with their most valuable part, by means of which there is produced, when a man chooses, fidelity, modesty, truth, law, a good daemon (happiness)?

To her who gives and takes back all, to nature, the man who is instructed and modest says, Give what thou wilt; take back what thou wilt. And he says this not proudly, but obediently and well pleased with her. Short is the little which remains to thee of life. Live as on a mountain. For it makes no difference whether a man lives there or here, if he lives everywhere in the world as in a state (political community).

Let men see, let them know a real man who lives according to nature. If they cannot endure him, let them kill him. For that is better than to live thus as men do. No longer talk at all about the kind of man that a good man ought to be, but be such. Constantly contemplate the whole of time and the whole of substance, and consider that all individual things as to substance are a grain of a fig, and as to time, the turning of a gimlet.

Book XI

These are the properties of the rational soul: it sees itself, analyses itself, and makes itself such as it chooses; the fruit which it bears itself enjoys- for the fruits of plants and that in animals which corresponds to fruits others enjoy- it obtains its own end, wherever the limit of life may be fixed. Not as in a dance and in a play and in such like things, where the whole action is incomplete, if anything cuts it short; but in every part and wherever it may be stopped, it makes what has been set before it full and complete, so that it can say, I have what is my own. And further it traverses the whole universe, and the surrounding vacuum, and surveys its form, and it extends itself into the infinity of time, and embraces and comprehends the periodical renovation of all things, and it comprehends that those who come after us will see nothing new, nor have those before us seen anything more, but in a manner he who is forty years old, if he has any understanding at all, has seen by virtue of the uniformity that prevails all things which have been and all that will be. This too is a property of the rational soul, love of one's neighbour, and truth and modesty, and to value nothing more than itself, which is also the property of Law. Thus then right reason differs not at all from the reason of justice.

Thou wilt set little value on pleasing song and dancing and the pancratium, if thou wilt distribute the melody of the voice into its several sounds, and ask thyself as to each, if thou art mastered by this; for thou wilt be prevented by shame from confessing it: and in the matter of dancing, if at each movement and attitude thou wilt do the same; and the like also in the matter of the pancratium. In all things, then, except virtue and the acts of virtue, remember to apply thyself to their several parts, and by this division to come to value them little: and apply this rule also to thy whole life.

What a soul that is which is ready, if at any moment it must be separated from the body, and ready either to be extinguished or dispersed or continue to exist; but so that this readiness comes from a man's own judgement, not from mere obstinacy, as with the Christians, but considerately and with dignity and in a way to persuade another, without tragic show.

Have I done something for the general interest? Well then I have had my reward. Let this always be present to thy mind, and never stop doing such good. What is thy art? To be good. And how is this accomplished well except by general principles, some about the nature of the universe, and others about the proper constitution of man?

At first tragedies were brought on the stage as means of reminding men of the things which happen to them, and that it is according to nature for things to happen so, and that, if you are delighted with what is shown on the stage, you should not be troubled with that which takes place on the larger stage.

For you see that these things must be accomplished thus, and that even they bear them who cry out "O Cithaeron." And, indeed, some things are said well by the dramatic writers, of which kind is the following especially:-

Me and my children if the gods neglect, This has its reason too. And again- We must not chale and fret at that which happens. And Life's harvest reap like the wheat's fruitful ear. And other things of the same kind.

After tragedy the old comedy was introduced, which had a magisterial freedom of speech, and by its very plainness of speaking was useful in reminding men to beware of insolence; and for this purpose too Diogenes used to take from these writers.

But as to the middle comedy which came next, observe what it was, and again, for what object the new comedy was introduced, which gradually sunk down into a mere mimic artifice. That some good things are said even by these writers, everybody knows: but the whole plan of such poetry and dramaturgy, to what end does it look!

How plain does it appear that there is not another condition of life so well suited for philosophising as this in which thou now happenest to be. A branch cut off from the adjacent branch must of necessity be cut off from the whole tree also.

Similarly, a man who separates from another male also loses contact with the entire social group. When a guy turns away from his neighbor out of hatred, he not only isolates himself from him but also cuts himself off from the entire social structure. However, a branch is chopped off by another person. He does, however, undoubtedly have this right since Zeus, who created society, gave us the ability to grow back to what is close to us and become a component that completes the entire.

However, if it often happens, this kind of separation, it makes it difficult for that which detaches itself to be brought to unity and to be restored to its former condition.

Finally, the branch, which from the first grew together with the tree, and has continued to have one life with it, is not like that which after being cut off is then engrafted, for this is something like what the gardeners mean when they say that it grows with the rest of the tree, but that it has not the same mind with it.

As those who try to stand in thy way when thou art proceeding according to right reason, will not be able to turn thee aside from thy proper action, so neither let them drive thee from thy benevolent feelings towards them, but be on thy guard equally in both matters, not only in the matter of steady judgement and action, but also in the matter of gentleness towards those who try to hinder or otherwise trouble thee.

For this also is a weakness, to be vexed at them, as well as to be diverted from thy course of action and to give way through fear; for both are equally deserters from their post, the man who does it through fear, and the man who is alienated from him who is by nature a kinsman and a friend.

Since the arts mimic nature, there is no nature that is less valuable than the arts. If this is the case, then nature—which is the most flawless and all-encompassing of all natures—cannot be inferior to the artistic ability. Since all forms of art now sacrifice the sublime for the sake of the lesser, universal nature likewise does this. Indeed, this is the source of justice, and it is from justice that the other virtues stem from.

This is because justice cannot be upheld if we are easily fooled, irresponsible, or changeable, or if we care about things that are in the middle.

If the things do not come to thee, the pursuits and avoidances of which disturb thee, still in a manner thou goest to them. Let then thy judgement about them be at rest, and they will remain quiet, and thou wilt not be seen either pursuing or avoiding.

The spherical form of the soul maintains its figure, when it is neither extended towards any object, nor contracted inwards, nor dispersed nor sinks down, but is illuminated by light, by which it sees the truth, the truth of all things and the truth that is in itself.

Consider whence each thing is come, and of what it consists, and into what it changes, and what kind of a thing it will be when it has changed, and that it will sustain no harm.

If any have offended against thee, consider first: What is my relation to men, and that we are made for one another; and in another respect, I was made to be set over them, as a ram over the flock or a bull over the herd. But examine the matter from first principles, from this: If all things are not mere atoms, it is nature which orders all things: if this is so, the inferior things exist for the sake of the superior, and these for the sake of one another.

Second, consider what kind of men they are at table, in bed, and so forth: and particularly, under what compulsions in respect of opinions they are; and as to their acts, consider with what pride they do what they do.

Third, that if men do rightly what they do, we ought not to be displeased; but if they do not right, it is plain that they do so involuntarily and in ignorance. For as every soul is unwillingly deprived of the truth, so also is it unwillingly deprived of the power of behaving to each man according to his deserts. Accordingly men are pained when they are called unjust, ungrateful, and greedy, and in a word wrong-doers to their neighbours.

Fourth, consider that thou also doest many things wrong, and that thou art a man like others; and even if thou dost abstain from certain faults, still thou hast the disposition to commit them, though either through cowardice, or concern about reputation, or some such mean motive, thou dost abstain from such faults.

Fifth, consider that thou dost not even understand whether men are doing wrong or not, for many things are done with a certain reference to circumstances. And in short, a man must learn a great deal to enable him to pass a correct judgement on another man's acts.

Sixth, consider when thou art much vexed or grieved, that man's life is only a moment, and after a short time we are all laid out dead.

Eighth, consider how much more pain is brought on us by the anger and vexation caused by such acts than by the acts themselves, at which we are angry and vexed.

Ninth, consider that a good disposition is invincible, if it be genuine, and not an affected smile and acting a part. For what will the most violent man do to thee, if thou continuest to be of a kind disposition towards him, and if, as opportunity offers, thou gently admonishest him and calmly correctest his errors at the very time when he is trying to do thee harm, saying, Not so, my child: we are constituted by nature for something else: I shall certainly not be injured, but thou art injuring thyself, my child.- And show him with gentle tact and by general principles that this is so, and that even bees do not do as he does, nor any animals which are formed by nature to be gregarious. And thou must do this neither with any double meaning nor in the way of reproach, but affectionately and without any rancour in thy soul; and not as if thou wert lecturing him, nor yet that any bystander may admire, but either when he is alone, and if others are present...

But if thou wilt, receive also a tenth present from the leader of the Muses (Apollo), and it is this that to expect bad men not to do wrong is madness, for he who expects this desires an impossibility. But to allow men to behave so to others, and to expect them not to do thee any wrong, is irrational and tyrannical.

There are four principal aberrations of the superior faculty against which thou shouldst be constantly on thy guard, and when thou hast detected them, thou shouldst wipe them out and say on each occasion thus: this thought is not necessary: this tends to destroy social union: this which thou art going to say comes not from the real thoughts; for thou shouldst consider it among the most absurd of things for a man not to speak from his real thoughts. But the fourth is when thou shalt reproach thyself for anything, for this is an evidence of the diviner part within thee being overpowered and yielding to the less honourable and to the perishable part, the body, and to its gross pleasures.

Book XII

All those things at which thou wishest to arrive by a circuitous road, thou canst have now, if thou dost not refuse them to thyself. And this means, if thou wilt take no notice of all the past, and trust the future to providence, and direct the present only conformably to piety and justice.

Conformably to piety, that thou mayest be content with the lot which is assigned to thee, for nature designed it for thee and thee for it. Conformably to justice, that thou mayest always speak the truth freely and without disguise, and do the things which are agreeable to law and according to the worth of each. And let neither another man's wickedness hinder thee, nor opinion nor voice, nor yet the sensations of the poor flesh which has grown about thee; for the passive part will look to this. If then, whatever the time may be when thou shalt be near to thy departure, neglecting everything else thou shalt respect only thy ruling faculty and the divinity within thee, and if thou shalt be afraid not because thou must some time cease to live, but if thou shalt fear never to have begun to live according to nature- then thou wilt be a man worthy of the universe which has produced thee, and thou wilt cease to be a stranger in thy native land, and to wonder at things which happen daily as if they were something unexpected, and to be dependent on this or that.

God sees the minds (ruling principles) of all men bared of the material vesture and rind and impurities. For with his intellectual part alone he touches the intelligence only which has flowed and been derived from himself into these bodies. And if thou also usest thyself to do this, thou wilt rid thyself of thy much trouble. For he who regards not the poor flesh which envelops him, surely will not trouble himself by looking after raiment and dwelling and fame and such like externals and show.

The things are three of which thou art composed, a little body, a little breath (life), intelligence. Of these the first two are thine, so far as it is thy duty to take care of them; but the third alone is properly thine.

Therefore if thou shalt separate from thyself, that is, from thy understanding, whatever others do or say, and whatever thou hast done or said thyself, and whatever future things trouble thee because they may happen, and whatever in the body which envelops thee or in the breath (life), which is by nature associated with the body, is attached to thee independent of thy will, and whatever the external circumfluent vortex whirls round, so that the intellectual power exempt from the things of fate can live pure and free by itself, doing what is just and accepting what happens and saying the truth: if thou wilt separate, I say, from this ruling faculty the things which are attached to it by the impressions of sense, and the things of time to come and of time that is past, and wilt make thyself like Empedocles' sphere, All round, and in its joyous rest reposing; and if thou shalt strive to live only what is really thy life, that is, the present- then thou wilt be able to pass that portion of life which remains for thee up to the time of thy death, free from perturbations, nobly, and obedient to thy own daemon (to the god that is within thee).

I have often wondered how it is that every man loves himself more than all the rest of men, but yet sets less value on his own opinion of himself than on the opinion of others. If then a god or a wise teacher should present himself to a man and bid him to think of nothing and to design nothing which he would not express as soon as he conceived it, he could not endure it even for a single day. So much more respect have we to what our neighbours shall think of us than to what we shall think of ourselves.

How can it be that the gods after having arranged all things well and benevolently for mankind, have overlooked this alone, that some men and very good men, and men who, as we may say, have had most communion with the divinity, and through pious acts and religious observances have been most intimate with the divinity, when they have once died should never exist again, but should be completely extinguished?

But if this is so, be assured that if it ought to have been otherwise, the gods would have done it. For if it were just, it would also be possible; and if it were according to nature, nature would have had it so. But because it is not so, if in fact it is not so, be thou convinced that it ought not to have been so: for thou seest even of thyself that in this inquiry thou art disputing with the deity; and we should not thus dispute with the gods, unless they were most excellent and most just;- but if this is so, they would not have allowed anything in the ordering of the universe to be neglected unjustly and irrationally.

Practice even the things that you are most afraid to accomplish. Because it has been practiced in this manner, even the left hand, which lacks practice in all other areas, holds the bridle with greater energy than the right. Think about the state a person should be in when death overtakes him, both physically and spiritually; also think about how brief life is, how infinitely long time spans can go by, and how frail all material things are.

Contemplate the formative principles (forms) of things bare of their coverings; the purposes of actions; consider what pain is, what pleasure is, and death, and fame; who is to himself the cause of his uneasiness; how no man is hindered by another; that everything is opinion.

In the application of thy principles thou must be like the pancratiast, not like the gladiator; for the gladiator lets fall the sword which he uses and is killed; but the other always has his hand, and needs to do nothing else than use it.

See what things are in themselves, dividing them into matter, form and purpose.

What a power man has to do nothing except what God will approve, and to accept all that God may give him. With respect to that which happens conformably to nature, we ought to blame neither gods, for they do nothing wrong either voluntarily or involuntarily, nor men, for they do nothing wrong except involuntarily.

Consequently we should blame nobody. How ridiculous and what a stranger he is who is surprised at anything which happens in life.

Chapter 1: Introduction to Marcus Aurelius and Stoicism

The Life of Marcus Aurelius

Marcus Aurelius Antoninus, celebrated for his lifelong dedication to philosophy and renowned among emperors for his unwavering commitment to a virtuous life, was born to Annius Verus, who held the position of praetor but passed away during his tenure. During Vespasian and Titus' term as censors, his grandfather, Annius Verus, achieved a second consulship, served as prefect of the city, and was honored with enrollment among the patricians. Annius Libo, his uncle, held the esteemed position of consul, while Galeria Faustina Augusta was his aunt. His mother, Domitia Lucilla, was the daughter of Calvisius Tullus, a distinguished individual who served as consul twice.

Annius Verus, from the town of Succuba in Spain, who was made a senator and attained to the dignity of praetor, was his father's grandfather; his great-grandfather on his mother's side was Catilius Severus, who twice held the consul-ship and was prefect of the city. His father's mother was Rupilia Faustina, the daughter of Rupilius Bonus, a man of consular rank.

Marcus pursued philosophy fervently from a young age. At twelve, he adopted the attire and lifestyle of a philosopher, later engaging in philosophical studies with Apollonius of Chalcedon and attending lectures by various Stoics and Peripatetics. He studied law under Lucius Volusius Maecianus and attended public rhetoric schools, forging strong friendships with several peers and showing generosity towards them.

Marcus received the equestrian rank at six and joined the Salii college, all under Hadrian's watchful supervision. As a college student, he showed early indications of future leadership and was given a major omen when, in the course of a usual ritual, his crown fell over Mars's brow. At fifteen he accepted manhood, courted the daughter of Lucius Ceionius Commodus at Hadrian's request, and performed admirably as city prefect at the Latin Festival. He was a man of great virtue; he even gave up his inherited wealth to help his sister, and he was a kind but severe man.

Upon Hadrian's death, Antoninus Pius succeeded him, and Marcus, despite his youth, was adopted into the Aurelian family. Subsequently, he was appointed quaestor and later ascended to the consulship alongside Pius. Marcus Aurelius married Faustina and, after the birth of a daughter, acquired significant powers and rights in governance. He held immense influence over Pius, advising on promotions and maintaining a respectful relationship despite gossip against him. Throughout these years, Marcus upheld his reputation with integrity and declined legacies, showing modesty and honor. For over two decades, he lived with his father in a manner that only deepened their bond.

Being forced by the senate to assume the government of the state after the death of the Deified Pius, Marcus made his brother his colleague in the empire, giving him the name Lucius Aurelius Verus Commodus and bestowing on him the titles Caesar and Augustus. Then they began to rule the state on equal terms, and then it was that the Roman Empire first had two emperors, when Marcus shared with another the empire he had inherited. He then adopted the name Antoninus for himself and gave Lucius Commodus the Verus and Antoninus namesake, acting as though he were the father of Lucius Commodus. He also engaged him to his daughter Lucilla, even though he was technically his brother. They issued orders to give girls and boys of newly named orders a portion in the grain distribution in honor of this union.

Following their duties in front of the Senate, the two emperors made their way to the praetorian camp, where they gave each common soldier twenty thousand sesterces and gave others awards based on their performance. They buried their father's body in the Tomb of Hadrian after conducting ornate funeral ceremonies. An official funeral procession paraded around the city after a holiday.

Both emperors recruited a college of Aurelian priests from their closest friends and gave eulogies for their father from the Rostra. They also appointed a priest from their own family.

As Verus reveled in Antioch and Daphne, participating in gladiatorial fights and hunting, Marcus kept a close eye on state matters, putting up with his brother's behavior but also supervising the carrying out of vital military preparations. Under Statius Priscus, the Armenian campaign was successful, and as a result, both emperors were given the honorary name Armeniacus, which Marcus first refused out of humility but eventually accepted. They were also both acclaimed as Parthicus, a title that Marcus first rejected before accepting.

Marcus placed a high priority on justice, upholding the laws governing property inheritance, inheritance taxes, and shielding people from extortion. He worked with jurists such as Scaevola and reinstated antiquated laws. He exercised the kind, generous, and forgiving governance of a free state, even in the face of irrationality. He made impartial decisions, resolved conflicts amicably and sympathetically, and avoided taking personal offense. He continued to operate in a reasonable but forceful manner.

Under Marcus's joint rule with Lucius Verus, the empire faced challenges, including natural disasters like severe flooding and a devastating famine, which the emperors addressed through personal involvement and aid.

Basic Principles of Stoicism

Stoicism is a living philosophy. What that means is that Stoic philosophy is more than just great thoughts organized into a complete and coherent vision of reality. It is first and foremost a philosophy to live by, a practical application of ancient wisdom, a way of life and a guide to the choices one makes in this life. And from its beginnings, it was the only philosophy addressed to all human beings – regardless of gender, race, or social class. Even women and slaves were welcome to follow this path, to be treated as sisters and brothers, a notion considered laughable by other philosophers who, along with Aristotle, classified them somewhere above brute beasts and below free men.

Stoicism is alive. The reason it is still alive after more than 2300 years is because it is universally adaptable and available to people of every color, class, and culture. And something else: it evolves. As the human race learns and grows, so does our philosophy. It evolves because of the strength and conviction of the Stoics themselves. Stoics have a tradition of independent thought, and we like it that way. We of the Stoic school do not follow a tyrant, as Seneca said. This is not to say that we have an eclectic hodgepodge of assorted ideas collected here and there. It is not. Its inner core of orthodoxy moves very slowly, glacially, expanding and refining with the ages.

Practice the Art of Living: Become a Warrior Philosopher

"First say to yourself what you would be; and then do what you have to do." — EPICTETUS

How to live a good life? This classic philosophic question stands at the origin of the primary concern of Stoic philosophy: How to live one's life, or "the art of living." Stoic teacher Epictetus compared philosophy to artisans: As wood is to the carpenter, and bronze to the sculptor, so are our own lives the proper material in the art of living.

Philosophy is not reserved for wise old men, it's an essential craft for everybody who wants to learn how to live (and die) well. Every life situation presents a blank canvas or a block of marble that we can sculpt and train on, so that over a lifetime we can master our craft. That's basically what Stoicism does, it teaches us how to excel in life, it prepares us to face adversity calmly, and simply helps us sculpt and enjoy a good life. What makes someone good at living? According to Epictetus, it's neither wealth, nor high-office, nor being a commander. There must be something else. Just like someone who wants to be good at handwriting must practice and know a lot about handwriting, or someone who wants to be good in music must study music, someone who wants to be good at living, therefore, must have good knowledge of how to live.

Eudaimonia

"Dig within. Within is the wellspring of Good; and it is always ready to bubble up, if you just dig." – MARCUS AURELIUS

The Stoics' overarching goal was eudaimonia; to be good with your inner daimon, to live in harmony with your ideal self, to express your highest version of yourself in every moment. But what does that mean exactly? The most common translation of the Greek word eudaimonia is happiness. The translations "flourishing" or "thriving," however, capture the original meaning better because they indicate a form of continuing action— you can only be good with your daimon when your moment-to-moment actions are in harmony with your ideal self. You flourish at living well, and only as a consequence you'll feel happy.

Emotional Resilience

"To bear trials with a calm mind robs misfortune of its strength and burden."– SENECA

"Unharmed prosperity cannot endure a single blow," says Seneca, but a man who has gone through countless misfortunes "acquires a skin calloused by suffering." This man fights to the ground and carries on the fight even on his knees. He will never give up. The Stoics loved wrestling metaphors, so Marcus Aurelius similarly says, "The art of living is more like wrestling than dancing." We need to be prepared for sudden attacks. Nobody will ever tackle a dancer. The dancer will never get choked by adversity like a wrestler. So, as warrior-philosophers, we know that life will be challenging. Actually, we should even be rubbing our hands together and be looking forward to take some punches, knowing they will make us stronger and grow our skin thicker. This is why we should want to engage and train in this fight they call life. Because we want to be strong, we want to live happy and smoothly flowing lives. We want to handle ourselves and our actions when life gets tough. We want to be a tower of strength, unshakable even at the peak of a rage attack. When others panic, we want to stay cool, well considered, and be able to be the best we can be.

Tame Restricting Emotions

The promise of Stoic philosophy consists of both the supremely happy life (eudaimonia) and the preparation (ready for anything) to deal effectively with whatever life throws at us. Yet, we can only deal well with life's challenges when we're emotionally resilient and don't let our emotions jerk us around. This is why we need to make progress toward taming and overcoming disturbing desires and emotions, so that, as Seneca puts it, the glitter of gold doesn't dazzle our eyes more than the flash o a sword, and that we can easily wave aside what other people crave and fear. This overcoming of one's emotions is sometimes called the Stoic "therapy of the passions" and might be the reason why Epictetus said: "The philosopher's school is a doctor's clinic."

Stoicism has nothing to do with suppressing or hiding one's emotions or being emotionless. Rather, it's about acknowledging our emotions, reflecting on what causes them, and learning to redirect them for our own good. In other words, it's more about liberating ourselves from negative emotions, more like taming rather than getting rid of them.

The Stoics want us to conquer our passions by becoming stronger than them and not by eliminating them. We will always feel the emerging emotional wolf, but we can train ourselves to recognize our tendency toward following along, and then deliberately choose whether to follow along or not. Stoicism will help us get less plagued by negative emotions and, at the same time, experience more positive emotions such as joy or tranquility. It's important to notice, however, that for the Stoics, these positive emotions are more like an added bonus than a motive by themselves.

Stoicism can be explained with these elements:

The Whole: A circle, representing the Whole that is greater than the sum of its parts, the One unifying all parts of reality, the Stoic deity as Nature. The Stoic God is the physical manifestation and processes of Nature. The universe is a living organism, and we are all creations of Nature. Each of us possesses a fragment of its intelligence and can rightly be called a son or daughter of God. As a panentheist, the deist Stoic holds that nature is a sentient, sentient whole that is greater than the sum of its parts. The pantheist who is an atheist, Stoic, holds that God is nothing more or less than the whole of its parts, and that God is merely a word that symbolizes the unconscious processes of nature. The skeptic or agnostic Stoic refuses to identify with one side. That's alright. The modern Stoic is welcome in our group whether they practice deism, atheism, or skepticism.

The Polarities: A diagonal line representing the connection of opposites, the Polarities, aka the dynamic continuum, which is essential for physical existence to occur. The natural world exists on a dynamic continuum of opposites. Depending on our personal preferences and views, the polarities of hot/cold, black/white, sweet/sour, life/death, and so forth may appear to humans to be good or terrible, but both ends of the continuum are required for life to exist in this material world. Nature is good; our perception of things determines whether they appear nice or bad. Evil does not exist in nature. Because only humans possess the capacity for reasoning to decide whether to evolve or degenerate morally over a single lifetime, only humans are capable of evil.

The Treasures: Three triangles representing the three Treasures of Beauty, Truth, and Love given to us by Nature to make life worth living and encourage virtue. Nature created us so that we could be aware of and appreciate life's greatest treasures – no matter how they may appear or what form they may take according to one's time and place in history. We are not drawn to hate, deception, or ugly things—the anti-treasures that are the reverse of treasures.

This teaches us about the goodness and will of Nature. From birth, every organism is endowed with a Primary Impulse that prioritizes self-preservation above everything else. Humans have the capacity to develop this self-love into altruism, or the love of others even at the expense of oneself. The path to virtue and the art of living is illuminated by our intrinsic attraction to the Treasures from birth and our innate repulsion to their opposites.

The Virtues: four lines of the square representing the four cardinal Virtues of Wisdom, Justice, Courage, and Decorum, the only good and the source of our noble character and happiness. It is from the Primary Impulse of self-love and our attraction to beauty and to the search for truth that we discover the highest good. That which is constantly good is the utmost good.

The only thing that can be considered the utmost good is virtue as it is included inside wisdom, as virtue is beneficial regardless of one's circumstances—healthy or ill, wealthy or impoverished. Wealth, power, and pleasure do not constitute the highest good because they might lead to unhappiness for oneself as well as for others. When the virtues are fully accepted, they result in an untouchable greatness of soul and noble character.

Chapter 2: Self-Control and Inner Discipline

Mastering Emotions

"Once [anger] begins to carry us away, it is hard to get back again into a healthy condition, because reason goes for nothing once passion has been admitted to the mind . . . The enemy must be met and driven back at the outermost frontier-line: for when he has once entered the city and passed its gates, he will not allow his prisoners to set bounds to his victory."

Happiness seems pretty doable, right? For the Stoics, it only consists in how we respond to events, and what we make of them. Aligning our actions with virtue is sufficient (but also necessary) for the happy and smoothly flowing life. So what happens? Why don't we all get there with a snap of the fingers?

Life has its snags. Life presents itself to us; it overwhelms us, takes us by surprise, instills feelings of fear, uncertainty, rage, and grief, and makes us want to hide and flee. Things are harder than we anticipated, and they transpire in ways that defy our hopes and expectations. We are finding it difficult to deal with them or simply to accept them as they are. But hold on! Stoicism emphasizes that we should seek out any good within ourselves and that external circumstances hold no significance.

It only seems that life gets in the way; in reality, it's our negative emotions that get in the way. These intense emotions conquer our mind, actually our whole being, make it impossible to think clearly, and urge us to do the opposite of what we think is right.

Once our mind has been captured by negative emotions, or passions as the Stoics call them, such as irrational fear, grief, anger, or greed, these passions take over, and we react impulsively without being able to think about it. As Seneca says in the opening lines to this chapter, once the enemy has entered the mind, reason is gone. It's one or the other, reason or passion; when passion is at the steering wheel, reason is tied up and gagged in the trunk.

Negative emotions naturally feel bad; think of grief, fear, jealousy, or strong cravings. So with the emotion in the driver's seat, and with something inside feeling bad, our number one priority (unconsciously) becomes to feel better, and we automatically seek relief of the pain we're feeling.

The negative feeling tells us to disregard our principles and long-term objectives in favor of doing whatever will make us feel better and ease our pain in the here and now.

Ultimately, we reject our core beliefs and choose to act cowardly by ordering pizza and tiramisu, binge-watching Marvel films, smashing doors and glassware, yelling at our friends and children, and purchasing those unnecessary black high heels.

Negative emotions can take countless forms. They can swallow us completely like intense anger which creates a sudden tunnel vision that simply lets us act out—bam!—and it's happened. They can be much calmer like excessive grief which can leave us full of self-pity, depressive thoughts, and complete inaction.

Which emotions come in the way doesn't really matter; for me, it's usually fear (I'm working on it), but for you, it may be pride, resentment, rage, or greed. The issue with these feelings is not that they exist, but rather that they overpower us and cause us to act against our better judgment. Furthermore, since our happiness stems from our logical behaviors, as we have previously learnt, we cannot be happy if we allow intense emotional disturbances to control our behavior.

It's essential to overcome these negative emotions if we want to practice Stoicism. This is why a key part of the Stoic philosophy is to prevent the onset of negative emotions, and to be prepared to deal with them effectively and not get overwhelmed if they arise nevertheless

"Passion is produced no otherwise than by a disappointment of one's desires." Epictetus makes the point that negative emotions arise when we don't get what we want. This disappointment "is the spring of sorrow, lamentation, and envy; this renders us envious and emulous, and incapable of hearing reason."

Basically, negative emotions come from wanting and fearing what's not under our control. As we learned earlier, the root cause of our suffering stems from worrying about stuff outside our control. These are flawed value judgments because we assign a positive or poor value to some neutral external object. For instance, the root of appetites for riches and pleasure is an incorrect assessment of material objects as desirable or good. Such intense cravings are caused by negative emotions that take control of our actions and allow us to act against our moral principles in order to temporarily satisfy our cravings. Remember, reason is gagged and tied up in the trunk because we are unable to hear it. Inaccurate value assessments sometimes have the opposite effect. When we incorrectly perceive a neutral external event—like rain, obnoxious individuals, or poverty—as awful or horrible, it might inspire anxiety or fury. Negative emotions are thus the result of making the incorrect assessment of an occurrence, and as such, they obstruct happiness by causing us to respond irrationally rather than sensibly.

Schedule breaks, treats, and rewards. Even the most disciplined mind needs rest to perform at its best. Plan time to relax, rest, socialize, and rejuvenate each day. Plan an indulgent meal, a day off from exercise, and breaks when working on a difficult project. The key is to plan these rewards in advance. Do not bargain with yourself when things get hard. Stick with your plan and know a reward is waiting when you are done.

Effectively learn from your mistakes. It is quite hard to break deeply ingrained habits quickly. Expecting too much might lead to disappointment and failure. Realize that success is about making progress rather than being flawless. Recognize the reason behind a setback, take lessons from it, and move on. As soon as you can, forgive yourself and get back on track.

Chapter 3: The Transitory Nature of Life Reflections on Death

Every human being goes through two basic experiences—first, the experience of life; and, then, the experience of death. If you seriously reflect on these two experiences, you are bound to discover the amazing fact that our having been sent into this world is not as a reward for anything, but, rather, for the purpose of an examination.

In this world, we think and feel that we are free. We have been given this freedom so as that it can be ascertained who among us has used this freedom properly and led a principled life, and who has not done so.

If you give that some serious thought, you'll see that dying marks the occasion when we must make our appearance before God. Although, as was previously indicated, we are truly everlasting beings, our lives are split into two stages: the pre-death and post-death phases. The aim of the former era is to test us, and the purpose of the latter is to reward or punish us based on the record of our deeds during the pre-death portion of our life. We now recognize ourselves as sentient, conscious entities. And when we pass away, we will be sent to the hereafter while we are still cognizant, alive creatures.

Each one of us is going to face that awesome day, sooner or later. It would be an unimaginably serious moment. Even after death we will remain the same beings as we were earlier, but everything that we possessed while on earth will have been stripped away from us forever. We will have left behind for good the world where we had spent the short pre-death period of our lives. In front of us another world will stretch, where we will have to live for eternity. A truly wise man is he who prepares himself adequately for this day

Every individual in this world is based on the "history" that we have created for ourselves. Everybody has access to many resources and possibilities, such as family, money, friends, fame, influence, power, and so forth, which they utilize to create their own unique "histories." Our identities are established by this "history" we write about ourselves; it is how we know ourselves and how others know us. Every one of us spends their entire lives working to accumulate our personal "history," which serves as the foundation for our sense of self. Yet, none of us gets to remain living in our 'history' for too long. Within a hundred years or so, death suddenly arrives and whisks us away. Death is a decision that cannot be revoked. It separates us from our pre-death period and takes us into the post-death period of our lives. In this sense, death can be said to mark a 'break' in our 'history'. In this world, we spend all our energies trying to build a little world of our own, a world of our many hopes and desires. All of us are living in these little worlds that we have ourselves constructed, till death carries us away.

Death forces us to leave our worlds behind and takes us into a different world, a world for which we may not have made any preparations at all. Behind us is the world we have left for good, and in front of us is an endless world, which we may not have been at all prepared for. Everybody has the chance to get ready for the eternal life that awaits them after death during the pre-death phase. You shall have to live in total deprivation during the afterlife if you use this chance only to pursue worldly pleasures and amass material prosperity. You will inevitably be separated from your pre-death "history"—all of the material possessions, reputation, and notoriety you had amassed.

Living in the Present Moment

If you look about you, you will see that everyone (including probably yourself, too) seems frantically busy with something or the other. People are so caught up doing things that they do not seem to have the time to listen to or think about anything else. They know of just one way of using their time and other resources—and that is, to spend it on seeking to achieve the numerous worldly goals they have set for themselves. People's business is geared simply to one thing. And that is, to make their little worlds as nice as possible. By and large, they are concerned only with worldly progress. Death, however, is a bold rebuttal of this worldview. Everyone has to die one day, and so all the worldly wealth you have accumulated will one day be snatched from you. You will have to leave behind forever the little world that you have spent all your energy, time and other resources in building. You will be taken towards such a world for which you possess nothing at all if you did not adequately prepare for it while in this world.

As soon as they are born, all individuals begin to think in the same terms as others around them. He becomes involved in a variety of materialistically driven activities, just like them. Consequently, materialism thought has permeated human history and continues to do so. It appears that no one can think without this kind of thinking these days, as it has become such an ingrained part of cultural customs. This is where the true test of man occurs. You need to start thinking independently and break free from this traditional style of thinking if you want to be genuinely successful in life.

You must separate yourself from traditional culture and thinking and form your opinions based on reality. If you do this, you will at once realize that the real issue for us human beings is not this-worldly progress, but, instead, preparation for the eternal Hereafter. Our real task is to prepare while in our pre-death period for the post-death period of our lives. We must work on developing ourselves in such a way that in the eternal life that will unfold after death we will be considered to be successful.

Everyone seems to be talking non-stop, doing this and that, being busy with all sorts of things, chasing all sorts of dreams. They are all driven with the purpose of trying to fulfil unlimited desires. They want to acquire all sorts of comforts for themselves and their children.

This is materialism's insane race. But what does it all amount to in the end? Everyone believes that their aspirations and goals have not been realized. People are therefore experiencing extreme desperation, resentment, stress, and frustration. They believe that what they want has been taken away from them. Nobody appears to be happy at all. This is how their days and nights go by in this terrible situation, until one day death carries them away and the small universe of their dreams collapses.

People are busy with things that belong to this temporary world, instead of preparing themselves for the eternal life after death. The life of this world is a test, and hence it is God's responsibility to provide every one of us with the things that we need to undergo this test. But as far as life after death is concerned, God has not taken responsibility for it.

Chapter 4: Virtue as the Supreme Good Definition of Virtue in Stoicism

Virtues are a reflection of life, and virtues originate from life. Before they recognize them as virtues, people play it out as life. The main goal of all ideas pertaining to virtues is to assist individuals in discovering the ultimate principles or secrets of happiness. Modern people are turning back to traditional ethical wisdom, like stoicism, in search of the practical wisdom of happiness because, despite their unending efforts, they are still so far from the path to happiness and so disenchanted with the myths surrounding the benefits of science and technology.

The most abstract wisdom regarding happiness tends to be the most practical and the most universal truth concerning happiness is also the most personal. The crisis of modernity has, undoubtedly, damaged and even ruined man's original oneness or harmony with nature and the inner universe of the heart. The moral aloneness and the deep sense of isolation have also led to the prevalent identity crisis. Both the sense of being and the sense of belonging have been gone with the wind. It is commonly acknowledged that" The social history of man started with his emerging from a state of oneness with the natural world to an awareness of himself as an entity separate from surrounding nature and men".

In the sphere of virtue ethics, men need to check the desires to some extent. Without a doubt, Stoicism can provide us with the essential source of moral power for the virtues. In some sense, Stoicism has supplied us with the eternal philosophically based wisdom with regard to the most significant and fundamental problems confronting mankind. With the modern society getting increasingly complicated and complex, we indeed need to be equipped with "the Stoic view of how to confront pain, disaster, and death without loss of peace of mind" so that we can truly build and cultivate the genuine and lasting virtues that serve as basic foundation of our sustainable happiness.

Stoicism unquestionably places a strong focus on ethics, namely on the central question of how each of us can lead a morally upright existence despite the unavoidable ups and downs of the world outside our minds. Although the Stoics sought contentment, they never imagined that true, long-lasting satisfaction could be found in the outside world or in obtaining external fame or fortune, as these things were not solely within our control. Generally speaking, there are two kinds of virtues. The first kind of virtue can be called the positive virtues, which provide us with the necessary mental and spiritual capacity to pursue the virtuous life. These positive virtues include courage, confidence, diligence, faith and so on. The other kind of virtues can be called negative virtues, such as temperance, discipline, self-control, tolerance, which, instead of motivating us to do something meaningful, remind us of the importance of not to do the morally bad things that can distract us from living the virtuous life with the peaceful mind.

According to the Stoics, "the chief end of man, and highest good, is happiness", and happiness is attained by" living according to Nature"." The Natural life, in fact, is the life controlled by reason; and such a life is briefly described as virtue". "It is this meaning of virtue which explains the Stoic dogma that virtue is the only good, and happiness consists exclusively in virtue." The fundamental reason why virtue is regarded as the only and highest good is simply because the so-called goods are never the good and the highest good is virtuously controlled by ourselves. The external things, no matter how many people regard them good, are never the highest good, because they are not up to ourselves, but are subjected to various external factors.

Exercises for Cultivating Virtue

Virtue is not an abiding possession or a permanent disposition for those who have cultivated and embraced it.

Virtue is based on the moral freedom to choose or the good, free, and moral will. The freedom of moral choice means the innate and firm soul force that can exercise the practical wisdom of life, regardless of the changes of outer circumstances. As Epictetus said," I must die: and must I die groaning too? Be fettered. Must it be lamenting too? Exiled. Can anyone prevent me, then, from going with a smile and good cheer and serenity? Betray the secret. I will not betray it; for this is in my own power. Then I will fetter you. What are you saying, man? Fetter me? You will fetter my leg; but not even Zeus himself can get the better of my choice. I will cast you into prison. My wretched body, rather. I will behead you. Did I ever tell you, that I alone had a head that can not be cut off? These are the things that philosophers ought to study; it is these that they should write about each day; and it is in these that they should exercise themselves." Since virtue resides in the moral freedom of the moral agents, the moral agents can guarantee that the ultimate happiness of his life is eventually up to himself. Therefore, he is able to overcome the sense of anxiety and helplessness caused by the dehumanizing aspect of the alienated modern society. Decent freedom fundamentally allows one to resist the world of senses, which is full with false promises of pleasure and temptations that can easily divert modern people from leading decent lives. In "our particular world in which conformity is the great destroyer of selfhood, in our society in which fitting the pattern tends to be accepted as the norm, and being well-liked is the alleged ticket to salvation," moral freedom to make decisions based on our good free will is what matters most in maintaining our individual identity.

While the capacity of human reason is limited, the capacity of human virtue is virtually unlimited. Stoicism has, in some sense, defended the integral dignity of virtues. There are two fundamental kinds of virtues, generally speaking, the positive virtues and the negative virtues.

Although one cannot conquer the entire globe, he can conquer the universe inside his own thoughts. Although man cannot control his circumstances, he is ethically able to choose how he will respond to those circumstances. Two types of sovereign powers that have the capacity to profoundly affect our moral disposition and conduct are pleasures and pains. Depending on our ability to regulate our attitudes toward our emotions, they have the potential to both increase our morals and have a detrimental impact on our virtues or personalities.

The truly virtuous people are the masters of their own emotions associated with what happen to them, and the vicious people are the slaves of their own emotions. Behind the virtue of self-control is the power of reason or rationality." To a rational creature, only what is contrary to reason is unendurable: but everything rational he can endure.""Blows are not by nature unendurable. How so? See how the Spartans bear a whipping, after they have learned that it is a reasonable thing."Similarly, virtues can never be separated from the power of reason or the power of rationality. It is just because of the existence of virtues that man can essentially become the true man.

"Since in our birth we have these two elements mingled within us, a body in common with the animals, and reason and intelligence in common with gods, many of us incline towards the former kinship, miserable as it is and wholly mortal, and only some few to the divine and blessed one."Without the conscious and active controlling of the negative side of human nature, or without the virtue of self-control serving as the gate-keeper of the emotions and human desires, it would be virtually impossible for the virtuous agents to live the virtuous life consistently.

The following crucial elements must be taken into account while discussing happiness: serenity, inner harmony, an uncluttered mind, and most importantly, a calm and serene mind. The basis of virtues is intimately related to each of the aforementioned important criteria. Although happiness is promised by virtues, this happiness is simply potential and must be achieved via good deeds and moral living.

Virtuous Happiness The economic activity and the wealth accumulated in the market economy, as well as the spreading of modern values such as equality, independence, freedom, love have enabled the modern people to reinforce their sense of individuality and uniqueness. However, the modern people have paid a high price for their individuality and freedom: the whole and traditional moral link between him and the larger social contexts has been irrevocably broken, leading to the desperate sense of being lonely and helpless. The mental security based on the traditional moral community is gone with the wind and the sense of belonging to the whole happiness social mechanism has also disappeared." Solidarity with one's fellow men, or at least with the members of one's own class, was replaced by a cynical detached attitude; other individuals were looked upon as objects to be used and manipulated. "The individual was absorbed by a passionate egocentricity, an insatiable greed for power and wealth."

Chapter 5: Reason and Logic Rationality in Stoic Ethics

Stoicism is known as a *eudaimonistic* theory, which means that the culmination of human endeavor or 'end' (*telos*) is *eudaimonia*, meaning very roughly "happiness" or "flourishing." The Stoics defined this end as "living in agreement with nature." "Nature" is a complex and multivalent concept for the Stoics, and so their definition of the goal or final end of human striving is very rich.

The first sense of the definition is living in accordance with nature as a whole, i.e. the entire cosmos. Cosmic nature (the universe), the Stoics firmly believed, is a rationally organized and well-ordered system, and indeed coextensive with the will of Zeus, the impersonal god. Consequently, all events that occur within the universe fit within a coherent, well-structured scheme that is providential. Since there is no room for chance within this rationally ordered system, the Stoics' metaphysical determinism further dictated that this cosmic Nature is identical to fate. Thus at this level, "living in agreement with nature" means conforming one's will with the sequence of events that are fated to occur in the rationally constituted universe, as providentially willed by Zeus.

In addition to basic metabolism, animals have the capacities of sense-perception, desire, and locomotion. Moreover, animals have an innate impulse to care for their offspring. Thus living in agreement with a creature's animality involves more complex behaviors than those of a plant living in agreement with its nature. For an animal parent to neglect its own offspring would therefore be for it to behave contrary to its nature. The Stoics believed that compared to other animals, human beings are neither the strongest, nor the fastest, nor the best swimmers, nor able to fly. Instead, the distinct and uniquely human capacity is reason. Thus for human beings, "living in agreement with nature" means living in agreement with our special, innate endowment—the ability to reason.

Theory of Appropriation

The Stoics developed a sophisticated psychological theory to explain how the advent of reason fundamentally transforms the world view of human beings as they mature. This is the theory of 'appropriation,' or *oikeiôsis*, a technical term which scholars have also translated variously as "orientation," "familiarization," "affinity," or "affiliation." The word means the recognition of something as one's own, as belonging to oneself. The opposite of *oikeiôsis* is *allotriôsis*, which neatly translates as "alienation." The Stoic notion of appropriation distinguishes between two developmental phases. As the competing Epicureans argue, self-love, not pleasure, is the innate, initial impulse of a living being, be it plant or animal, in the first stage. The organism is conscious of its own makeup, but in a more rudimentary way in plants than in animals. Its instant perception of its own body as "belonging to" itself is a component of this consciousness. Thus, the creature's goal is to preserve its constitution in its correct, or natural, state. As a consequence, the organism is impelled to preserve itself by pursuing things that promote its own well-being and by avoiding things harmful to it. Pleasure is only a by-product of success in this activity. In the case of a human infant, for example, appropriation explains why the baby seeks his mother's milk. But as the child matures, his constitution evolves.

Good, Evil, and Indifferent

The Stoics defined the good as "what is complete according to nature for a rational being qua rational being"

As explained above, the perfected nature of a rational being is precisely the perfection of reason, and the perfection of reason is virtue. The Stoics maintained, quite controversially among ancient ethical thought, that the only thing that always contributes to happiness, as its necessary and sufficient condition, is virtue. In contrast, the perversion of reason, namely vice, is the only thing that demands suffering and is considered "bad" or "evil". Everything else was classified as "indifferent" and was neither deemed good nor wicked. Because the Stoics believed that these goods neither enhance nor diminish a happy life, they were dubbed "indifferents." Since indifferents can be applied both poorly and well, they neither help nor hurt.

The four primary categories of virtue identified by the Stoics are wisdom, justice, courage, and moderation. They also developed a thorough taxonomy of virtue. Good sense, sound judgment, rapid thinking, discretion, and resourcefulness are the several categories of wisdom. The categories of justice include equity, fair dealing, piety, and honesty. The qualities of endurance, confidence, high-mindedness, cheerfulness, and diligence are the divisions of courage. Moderation can be further classified as self-control, humility, seemliness, and good discipline.

The Stoics categorize vices into groups according to similar categories: intemperance, folly, injustice, and cowardice. The Stoics further maintained that the virtues are inter-entailing and constitute a unity: to have one is to have them all. They held that the same virtuous mind is wise, just, courageous, and moderate. Thus, the virtuous person is disposed in a certain way with respect to each of the individual virtues. To support their doctrine of the unity of virtue, the Stoics offered an analogy: just as someone is both a poet and an orator and a general but is still one individual, so too the virtues are unified but apply to different spheres of action.

Appropriate Acts and Perfect Acts

Once a human being has developed reason, his function is to perform "appropriate acts" or "proper functions." The Stoics defined an appropriate act as "that which reason persuades one to do" or "that which when done admits of reasonable justification". Maintaining one's health is given as an example. Since health is neither good nor bad in itself, but rather is capable of being used well or badly, opting to maintain one's health by, say, walking, must harmonize with all other actions the agent performs. Similarly, sacrificing one's property is an example of an act that is only appropriate under certain circumstances. The observance of proper behavior is merely a prerequisite for virtue; it is not a sufficient one. This is due to the fact that the agent ought to comprehend the actions he takes correctly. In particular, his decisions and denials must combine to create a seamless sequence of deeds that concurrently upholds all of the qualities. Every action embodies the entirety and coherence of his moral rectitude. The great majority of individuals lack virtue because, while they may act morally when they respect their parents, for example, they do not abide by "the laws of life as a whole" by acting morally when it comes to the other virtues.

The virtuous person is not passionless in the sense of being unfeeling like a statue. Rather, he mindfully distinguishes what makes a difference to his happiness—virtue and vice—from what does not. This firm and consistent understanding keeps the ups and downs of his life from spinning into the psychic disturbances or "pathologies" the Stoics understood passions to be.

The early Stoics were fond of uncompromising dichotomies—all who are not wise are fools, all who are not free are slaves, all who are not virtuous are vicious, etc. The later Stoics distinguished within the class of fools between those making progress and those who are not.

Chapter 6: The Universe and Our Part in It- Marcus Aurelius' Cosmological View

Stoicism, as a philosophy, views the universe as a rational and harmonious entity governed by divine reason or logos. Marcus Aurelius embraced this Stoic worldview, which emphasized living in accordance with nature, accepting the order of the cosmos, and recognizing one's place within it. According to Stoic cosmology, the universe is a rational and interconnected system where everything is interdependent and follows a predetermined order. Marcus Aurelius believed in the concept of 'sympatheia' or sympathy, suggesting that everything in the universe is connected, and each part influences the whole.

The universe operates according to a grand design, and individuals should align their lives with this cosmic order to attain tranquility and inner peace.

Acceptance and Harmony with the Cosmos

Marcus and other Stoic thinkers made significant contributions to political philosophy that centered on the city-state as the primary setting for communal life. Small, patriotic city-states served as the normative paradigm for their ideas. Both thinkers assumed that the population of an ideal community would be small, not much more than six figures. They saw both offensive and defensive conflicts as sporadic needs. For example, Aristotle thought that Babylon was too big to be a true city-state even with its surrounding walls.

However, Stoic ethical and political thought diverged from this perspective over five centuries. It embraced cosmopolitanism in various forms. Influential figures like Crates of Thebes, a leading Cynic follower of Diogenes, significantly influenced Zeno, the Cypriot immigrant who established the Stoic school of philosophy in Athens.

Notable personalities like the Roman jurist Cicero, the apostle Paul, Philo, the Alexandrian exegete of the Torah, and the Roman emperor Marcus Aurelius expressed cosmopolitan sentiments. Philo, although not officially a Stoic adherent, incorporated Stoic ideas into his interpretations of the Torah. Marcus Aurelius, during his reign, advocated for a universal sense of citizenship.

The timeless cosmopolitan ideas of the ancient Stoics are still relevant today. Natural law theory, Kantian moral universalism, and the notion of a person's worthlessness in relation to their gender, color, or status are all echoed by their beliefs. Nonetheless, contemporary conceptions of cosmopolitanism are very different, placing a strong emphasis on free trade, supranational initiatives to bring about global peace and lessen suffering across national borders, and international political institutions.

The concept of "citizen of the world" in ancient times differed from the modern interpretation. While a literal world citizenship was impossible due to the absence of a global state, Stoic cosmopolitans encouraged treating all individuals, regardless of their origin or location, as quasi-siblings. They advocated for fair treatment and care for fellow humans solely based on the shared identity of being human.

The ancient concept of world citizenship operated alongside traditional cities, characterized by specific territorial boundaries, cultural traditions, laws, political institutions, and social identities. In Homer's epic poetry, the absence of full-fledged cities in the narrative points to a different structure of communities. Homer's evenhandedness in portraying different sets of people implies an ethical orientation that transcends ethnic and national identities.

While Homer's outlook hints at cosmopolitanism, it doesn't fully transcend nationalism. The absence of the word "barbarian" in reference to non-Greeks in his works indicates a lack of strong nationalism. However, prejudices against non-Greeks gained traction later, especially during Athens' hegemony over other Greek city-states.

Stoic philosophy profoundly influenced the cosmopolitan sentiments prevailing in later antiquity. Examples abound, such as the Apostle Paul's Epistle to the Galatians (3:26), where he emphasizes the unity in Christ by transcending distinctions of race, status, and gender. This echoes Marcus Aurelius's notion of universal citizenship, aligning with Stoic principles that underscore the fundamental equality of all human beings based on their inherent attributes.

Chapter 7: The Importance of Self-Reflection Writing for Personal Growth

Reflection and self-assessment are both meaningful processes that can lead to learning from experience, yet they have different purposes and goals. Reflection is a process that involves playing back a period of time related to previous valued experiences in search of significant discoveries or insights about oneself, one's behaviors, one's values, or knowledge gained. Specific criteria for performance are usually not involved. An important goal in reflection is bringing focus to an indeterminate situation by gaining clarity and by fully experiencing what has happened. It is important to gain closure during reflection and not ruminate repeatedly about the experience. Reflection involves divergent thinking and often includes journaling. In contrast, self-assessment is a process used for studying one's own performance in order to improve it. It is more proactive than reflection in that performance criteria are defined before the action in question begins or before it is replayed; and strengths, improvements, and insights against these criteria are then recorded during the process.

Self-knowledge is at the core of an emotionally healthy person. Healthy people have taken the time to look inside themselves to see what is really there. They are better able to question traditional assumptions and take charge where needed. They are more likely to engage in positive relationships, both in the work place and in their personal lives. They are able to call upon a variety of coping mechanisms, not just the ones that have been instilled in them by others. An ability to observe our own actions, be active instead of passive, and be fully aware of the various pressures on us (such as family and cultural influences and gender role expectations) can give us greater self-esteem and help us handle difficult circumstances. The ability to step outside of ourselves and observe who we are with objectivity is important for good mental health. In psychotherapy, this is called "the observing ego." Much of therapy is devoted to helping patients cultivate a greater ability to see who they are without being totally immersed in that self.

The more we can sort out who we really are (our core personality and beliefs) from the person others expect or want us to be, the more authentic we will be in our lives, and the more joy and purposefulness we are likely to develop. As we examine ourselves, we may find that we are changing from what we used to be into something else. Sometimes in the midst of that change, we find ourselves confused about our identity. We grapple in different ways with the concept of the "self"— that part of us that is both permanent yet changeable. We ask ourselves the question: If my identity is stable, then how does it change? If it is temporary, then who am I over time? How do I retain a coherent sense of self if I am changing? And, finally, do I really want to change? There is an inherent tension between the consistency of the self and the fact that the self can change. Too much consistency produces a person who is not flexible and cannot learn from his or her environment.

Too much fluctuation produces someone who does not have a solid sense of self, which can interfere with productive functioning. So many of us want to hold on to the self we know, and are afraid to explore it for fear it might change—yet change is exactly what we need. To rephrase an old saying, sometimes "it's the angel that you don't know rather than the devil you know" that awaits you if you have the courage to risk some changes.

Turning Points and Key People

Our family traditions (including cultural influences) are also basic determinants of who we turn out to be. Because we are born into these traditions, we may not understand how much they affect our sense of self until we are able to take a step back and assess them objectively.

People outside our families can also have an influence on our lives. These people may include friends, teachers, supervisors, mentors, adversaries, and political or religious figures. Their influence can be subtle or obvious, negative or positive, and sometimes both. We can be changed by things that they say or do to us. On a more subtle level, the way these people interact with the world in general can serve as a model for us. We observe what others do and incorporate that experience into our world view.

Chapter 8: Society and Ethics Social and Political Responsibilities

The adjective "social" has a number of meanings. The moral responsibilities to which we alluded earlier are social insofar as they arise from relationships between people. For example, the sale of a faulty product that may harm consumers gives rise to the obligation to compensate for this harm. However, SR has acquired a broader meaning. In the example given above, it establishes a generic consumer entitlement to safe products and a responsibility that applies to all companies, beyond the specific relationship between a buyer and a seller. It is responsibility to all of society (although on occasions it is limited to a group of stakeholders), and this is reflected in many definitions of SR, with phrases such as: "integrate social and environmental concerns," "contribute to a better society," "respect people, communities and the environment," and "treat the stakeholders in a socially responsible manner."

Political and social responsibilities are related aspects that define what people and things owe to society and the government. The ethical responsibilities that people and companies have to the environment and the community are embodied in social responsibility. It includes a broad range of activities, such as charity projects meant to promote the welfare of society and sustainable corporate practices. Furthermore, social responsibility emphasizes taking a proactive stance in addressing urgent social concerns including reducing poverty, ensuring access to education, and maintaining the environment. It goes beyond simply abiding by rules and regulations.

On the other hand, political responsibility pertains to the duty of citizens and governing bodies to contribute positively to the political process and the governance of a nation. It involves exercising rights judiciously, participating in democratic processes, and holding elected officials accountable.

Political responsibility underscores the significance of civic engagement, informed decision-making, and the ethical use of power by policymakers and institutions to serve the greater good and uphold democratic values.

A healthy and balanced society is built on the interconnectedness of social and political duties. For the benefit of both the current and future generations, they demand our shared commitment to bringing about constructive change and guaranteeing justice, fairness, and sustainable development. When people and organizations take on these obligations, they significantly contribute to the development of just societies and democratic government.

Beyond elections, political responsibility demands active engagement in the democratic process, which includes promoting policy changes, having polite conversations, and upholding the law.

It highlights how crucial it is to support the values of justice, accountability, and openness in governance while promoting communication and understanding amongst people of different beliefs. Honoring political obligations by individuals and leaders fortifies democracy and promotes a society where the common good is given precedence above personal gain, leading to more just and equal communities. Therefore, it is assumed that, when society voices its requirements, demands, claims or expectations, it is formulating potential or effective rights that deserve public recognition. (Even those that are recognized only for certain groups still have the support of the community.)

The strength of these demands comes from various sources: coercion (by society or by the state), ethics (either because the recognized right implies a moral duty or because a normative value is bestowed on what society proposes), convenience (the organization agrees to negotiate its responsibilities), etc. Society also demands that organizations be accountable for their commitments, the means they have used or will use to meet them, and the results, which enables a certain degree of control to be maintained. This modern conception of SR has its roots in profound changes in society, ideas or ideologies, with major consequences:

In postmodern society, rights have proliferated. They have become changing and relative, and attempts are often made to turn mere preferences into formal rights. This inflation of rights translates into a proliferation of SR demands.

The wording of these rights is often ambiguous – for example, when it is said that the firm needs a "social license" to operate (without it being known who grants it and under what terms and what its effects are) or that the firm must "give back" to society what it has received (without it being specified how this is to be calculated) or that, as a "good citizen," the firm must help improve society, or that it must make good use of its power.

Society is an abstract body that encompasses many groups (politicians, government officials, academics, companies, the media, civil society organizations) with different interests that compete for the attention of the state (to validate their demands) and for the attention of firms (to get them to accept their responsibilities).

Society operates as a complex web of interactions and relationships between various entities, each holding its own stake and agenda. Politicians and government officials are entrusted with representing public interests and shaping policies that cater to the needs of their constituents. Meanwhile, academia plays a pivotal role in generating knowledge, critical thinking, and innovative solutions, contributing significantly to societal progress and development.

Companies and the media, on the other hand, hold significant influence in shaping public opinion, societal values, and economic activities, thereby assuming responsibilities that extend beyond their immediate interests.

There is some tension in the interactions between these groups. Conflicting interests frequently lead to difficulties that could impede success as a group. It takes teamwork, consensus-building, and a dedication to finding common ground to balance these disparate interests while attending to the demands of society as a whole. These organizations can work together to create a more successful and cohesive community by acknowledging their shared societal duties and creating an atmosphere that promotes development, creativity, and social harmony.

Chapter 9: Suffering and Adversity Facing Life's Trials Finding Strength in Difficulties

An inevitable aspect of being human is suffering, and misfortune frequently strikes without warning, testing our resiliency and bravery. The Roman Emperor and Stoic philosopher Marcus Aurelius discussed the inevitable nature of hardships in life, drawing on the principles of Stoic philosophy, which emphasize bearing difficulty with calm and reason. He believed that hardship is a chance for human development and that the degree of character and resilience that a person develops depends on how they handle adversity. In a same vein, accepting that hardships are a natural part of life necessitates overcoming them.

Stoic teachings emphasize the importance of maintaining an inner sanctuary of peace amidst external turmoil. Epictetus, another influential Stoic philosopher, highlighted the power of perception in navigating hardships. He advocated for acknowledging challenges as opportunities for personal development, emphasizing the significance of controlling one's reactions to adversity. By focusing on what lies within our control, such as our thoughts and actions, rather than external circumstances, individuals can find strength and resilience in the face of life's trials.

When confronted with adversity, individuals often discover hidden reservoirs of resilience. Psychological research underscores the human capacity to adapt and find meaning in the midst of suffering. Holocaust survivor and psychologist Viktor Frankl claimed that people are free to decide how to react, even in the most difficult situations. Finding meaning and purpose in the midst of extreme suffering is stressed by Frankl's existential approach as a source of inner strength. When faced with adversity with a growth perspective, it can be a catalyst for personal progress.

Difficulties provide insightful lessons and chances for introspection, inspiring people to develop resilience, fortitude, and a better sense of self. Gaining knowledge from setbacks frequently results in personal growth and increases resilience and flexibility.

Perseverance and hope are essential for overcoming hardship and navigating life's challenges. Resilience is the capacity to bear hardships with a positive attitude. Narratives of people who have triumphed against overwhelming challenges frequently serve as motivational examples of the human spirit's enduring resilience. In difficult times, hope serves as a lighthouse, giving people the courage and willpower to persevere in the face of difficulty. Hope, whether it comes from one's own convictions, philosophies, or the encouragement of others, is a motivating factor that helps people get through challenging times.

Adversity and challenges are an inevitable part of life, yet they offer a profound opportunity for personal growth and resilience. When faced with difficulties, individuals often discover untapped reservoirs of strength within themselves. These moments of struggle serve as catalysts for self-discovery and the cultivation of inner fortitude. Every hurdle surmounted and every disappointment avoided helps people become more resilient, which empowers them to face obstacles in the future with more assurance and insight.

Furthermore, challenges frequently serve as a teacher, offering priceless lessons that mold perspective and character.

People frequently acquire remarkable insights into their own strengths and limitations when faced with hardship. Adversity offers a distinct perspective that enables people to reevaluate their priorities, hone their problem-solving abilities, and cultivate a more profound comprehension of their own principles and convictions. One frequently finds the will and resolve to push through these difficult times, calling on an inner power that could have lain dormant in other circumstances.

Moments of hardship are not just individual trials; they also foster empathy and compassion for others enduring similar struggles. Shared experiences of adversity create connections and build bonds, fostering a sense of camaraderie and support among people facing similar challenges. In overcoming personal difficulties, individuals often find themselves in a better position to empathize with and provide guidance and support to others navigating their own paths through adversity. This mutual understanding and empathy contribute to the strength of communities and societies as a whole, offering a collective resilience that helps everyone weather life's storms.

Finding strength in difficulties often involves striking a delicate balance between acceptance and resilience. While acceptance acknowledges the reality of challenges, resilience fuels the determination to navigate through them. It is the fusion of these qualities that enables individuals to confront adversity with grace and fortitude. This dynamic interplay empowers individuals to face life's trials with a sense of realism while maintaining the resolve to emerge stronger from the experience. In embracing this equilibrium, individuals cultivate the capacity to withstand hardships without losing sight of their inherent ability to endure and thrive.

Adversity not only helps people become resilient, but it also acts as a potent spark for creativity and invention. When faced with difficulties, people frequently have to think creatively and consider novel approaches to problems in order to find solutions.

The Roman Emperor and Stoic philosopher Marcus Aurelius left behind a plethora of knowledge that is consistent with the idea of finding strength in adversity. Aurelius discussed the benefits of resilience in his influential work "Meditations," highlighting the significance of meeting obstacles head-on. Adversities, in his opinion, are not things to be avoided but rather chances for development and education. Aurelius advocated for the development of inner strength and fortitude to withstand life's challenges, emphasizing that one's response to hardships mattered more than the hardships themselves.

Chapter 10: Inner Freedom Independence from the Material Inner Peace

Freedom is defined from different aspects, and according to different cultures, freedom varies from culture to another. Some define freedom as a natural right, the human being is born with. Everyone wants to be free and independent from others. Freedom is the right to do what one wants, live where he wants, eat what he wants, learns what he wants, and chooses the religion in which he believes, without ignoring or harming other rights. Freedom, independence, liberty refer to an absence of undue restrictions and an opportunity to exercise one's rights and powers. Freedom emphasizes the opportunity given for the exercise of one's rights, powers, desires, or the like: freedom of speech or conscience; freedom of movement. Independence implies not only lack of restrictions but also the ability to stand alone, unsustained by anything else: Independence of thought promotes invention and discovery. Liberty, though most often interchanged with freedom, is also used to imply undue exercise of freedom.

Aurelius stressed that a trained mind and a conscious disengagement from outside influences are necessary steps on the way to inner liberation. Stoicism emphasised the value of distinguishing between one's controllable and uncontrollable circumstances.

This way of thinking advised people to avoid getting involved in situations that were out of their control and to spend all of their attention and energy on managing their attitudes, beliefs, and behaviors. Aurelius felt that people may achieve a condition of calm and inner serenity by cultivating this self-mastery, independent of outside chaos or limitations.

All normal human beings are born and remain free in the most important sense that they are forever and at every conscious moment freely-choosing beings, and every life is a delicate tapestry of millions of such personal choices, for better or worse. We cannot escape this kind of freedom even if we try, for we must then freely choose among means of escape, and so on. From this perspective we are condemned to be free, for even choosing not to choose is a choice. Internal freedom is of the greatest personal intimacy and secretiveness, indeed it is the hidden core of our being and unknowable by others. It distinguishes human beings from the animal kingdom, and from each other, and is the basis on which we are able to become moral - or a-moral, or immoral - beings. That is why some people call this moral freedom. But this kind of freedom is not in itself moral. Rather, it is the unique capacity we have to become moral or immoral according to how we use our freedom.

Inner freedom is an intrinsic state of being that transcends external circumstances and arises from a profound sense of self-awareness and mental resilience. It involves liberating oneself from the shackles of limiting beliefs, fears, and external influences that hinder personal growth and fulfillment.

In order to develop a sense of autonomy and independence from outside validations or societal standards, achieving inner freedom necessitates a thorough examination of one's thoughts, emotions, and reactions to diverse situations. When faced with unforeseen or adverse situations, people can break free from the grip of worry or despair by adopting a more adaptable and flexible outlook. Because of their resilience, they are able to withstand life's inevitable ups and downs and maintain a sense of inner serenity and stability.

Frequent self-reflection helps one better comprehend themselves, identify their feelings, and ascertain the real purpose of outside occurrences. People can better understand their emotions, prejudices, and wants through this introspective trip, which gives them the ability to make deliberate decisions that are consistent with their values rather than giving in to rash or unreasonable impulses. By becoming more self-aware, people can transcend the influence of transient feelings and outside forces and develop a stronger sense of inner freedom.

This understanding of impermanence promotes resilience and a sense of emancipation, empowering people to confront obstacles in life with greater openness and composure.

Being materially independent indicates that one values experiences, relationships, and personal development more than accumulating material belongings. It includes consciously stepping back from looking to material money or goods as the main means of achieving contentment or happiness.

Deciding to give up material belongings is acknowledging that they are ephemeral and frequently do not bring to long-term satisfaction. It involves reorienting one's priorities from material possessions to things that actually bring true happiness, such meaningful relationships, growth, and life-enriching experiences.

The Stoic principles upheld by Marcus Aurelius echoed the notion that inner freedom comes from reducing one's reliance on external factors, especially material possessions. Aurelius encouraged individuals to liberate themselves from the insatiable desire for more, recognizing that the pursuit of material wealth often leads to discontentment and a perpetual cycle of longing. According to his teachings, inner peace is found not in the accumulation of material goods but in the practice of self-discipline, resilience, and the acceptance of life's inherent uncertainties. By embracing simplicity and minimizing reliance on external things for contentment, one can achieve a deeper sense of inner freedom.

Chapter 11: Friendship and Relationships, The Role of Friendship in Stoicism Interpersonal Conduct

Stoicism is a curious philosophy. At its core is the strong conviction that we need nothing and need no one to be happy. Epictetus clearly summarizes this conviction. Sick and yet happy, in danger and yet happy; dying and yet happy; condemned to exile and yet happy; lost his reputation and yet happy. (Epictetus, Discourses 2.19) So a Stoic needs nothing that the outside world can give her. She is self-sufficient—doesn't need wealth, health or even life itself; doesn't need company; and certainly doesn't need other people's approval.

The curious part is this. In Stoicism, the term 'preferred indifferent' is not an oxymoron, but a guiding principle. Stoics may not need any of the 'good things' others have, but they would rather have these than not. The Cynics, who came before the Stoics, made no such distinction between the two. They had no reason to want what they didn't need. The Stoics softened their approach by introducing the concept of preferred indifferents. You are free to enjoy anything that life may offer you, as long as the payment for it does not include compromising your virtues. As I said earlier, the concept of preferred indifferents is not an oxymoron in Stoicism. The Stoics point out that we are free to acquire and enjoy wealth as long as the price we pay for it does not include stupidity, cowardice, excessiveness, and injustice. This enabled them to 'want' things that they did not 'need,' leading to statements like these:

Is health 'good'? Health is good when used well and bad when used ill. (Epictetus, Discourses 3.20)

Is poverty 'bad'? It is not poverty that we should reject, but our judgment regarding it, and then we shall be at peace. (Epictetus, Discourses 3.20) Now that's settled, where do the Stoics stand on friendship? Like they stand on anything external. Friendship is a highly preferred indifferent. It is something you can live without, but life is better with it.

Friendship held a significant role in Stoicism, reflecting a fundamental aspect of human nature and social interaction. Stoic philosophers, including Marcus Aurelius and Seneca, underscored the importance of cultivating meaningful relationships based on virtues, mutual respect, and shared values. According to Stoic principles, friendships grounded in virtues, rather than mere pleasure or utility, were highly regarded as essential for personal growth and moral development. The Stoics believed that authentic friendships contribute to emotional well-being and serve as a support system during life's trials and tribulations.

Stoicism regarded friendships as a means to practice virtues and maintain emotional equilibrium. Stoic philosophers encouraged individuals to forge relationships not for personal gain but for the sake of shared growth and moral support.

A genuine friendship in Stoicism was seen as a harmonious bond where individuals learn from each other, practice empathy, and reinforce Stoic values through mutual encouragement and guidance. Emphasizing the quality of friendships over quantity, Stoicism recognized the role of companionship in fostering resilience, inner strength, and the pursuit of a virtuous life.

Thus, Marcus sees nothing wrong with fake friendship. We shouldn't be angry since ignorance is the source of false friendships. Generally speaking, stoics see friendship as a component of a greater whole. We forgive the transgressions of others because it is in our nature to be global citizens and members of the human race. These people are our brothers and sisters. In any case, since they are external to us, the sins of others cannot impact us.

Friendship is about giving rather than receiving. Here's one additional conundrum. If we don't think we'll get anything from our friendships, then why do we establish them? What keeps us friends if the benefits stop coming if we do become friends because we profit from them? According to Seneca, friendship is about giving rather than receiving. So why do I choose to become friends with men?

To have someone to die for, to go into exile with, to stake my own life against, and to pay the pledge for their death. (Seneca, On Friendship and Philosophy, Moral Letters) This idea is intriguing.

Here, we are not warily searching for "friends" with hidden agendas, as we truly don't require anything from people. Instead, we become friends with them to better their life. We might gain anything in return as we help our pals. If not, it is completely irrelevant. We are not pursuing it since it is external.

Friendship is a two-way street. However, friendships cannot exist without discrimination. If someone is your friend, you ought to have complete faith in him. As such, you ought to exercise extreme caution when selecting a friend. Consider carefully before accepting a particular person into your friendship, but once you have made the decision to do so, give him a warm welcome. Talk to him as brashly as you talk to yourself. Treat him with loyalty, and you'll win his loyalty.

In brief:

1. Stoics don't need friendship and yet value it. Stoics realize that they are a part of a larger society.
2. Stoics are not offended when a friend betrays them. And yet, Stoics choose their friends with great care and trusts them implicitly.
3. Stoics care about what they can do for their friend rather the other way around. Friendship in the time of Covid Generally, we take for granted our relationship with others, including our friendships. If we set aside our Facebook 'friends' for now, our current situation does not permit us as much contact with our friends as we would like. When our contact with others become limited, as is the case now, our thoughts return to our relationship with others, including our friends. What should friendship mean to us? Seek the company of those who uplift you.

Only spend time with positive people who inspire you and motivate you to perform at your highest level. Although there is merit to passing acquaintances formed by shared interests, we have all heard of individuals who were destroyed by "running with a bad crowd." Thus, it pays to pick our friends wisely. See this as a chance to cultivate your own virtue.

Chapter 12: Leadership and Power Marcus Aurelius as a Stoic Emperor

Marcus Aurelius, the Roman Emperor from 161 to 180 AD, is renowned for his deep association with Stoic philosophy and his adherence to its principles during his rule. As a Stoic emperor, Marcus Aurelius exemplified the philosophical virtues espoused by Stoicism, emphasizing self-discipline, rationality, and a commitment to moral goodness. His reign was marked by a profound dedication to justice, wisdom, and the pursuit of virtue as guiding principles for governance, drawing heavily from Stoic teachings in his leadership style.

Marcus Aurelius's Stoic approach to governance emphasized the alignment of personal virtues with the responsibilities of leadership. He prioritized the welfare of his people, seeking to rule with fairness, compassion, and humility. His reign was characterized by efforts to maintain stability, promote social welfare, and administer justice impartially. Marcus Aurelius's embodiment of Stoic principles in his role as an emperor has left a lasting legacy, inspiring generations with his philosophical reflections on ethics, duty, and the harmonious integration of personal virtue with the exercise of power.

When leaders practice such self-integrity as a part of their daily refection, they can avoid falling prey to many pitfalls born of self-obliviousness and cluelessness that lead to their downfall. Likewise, reviewing the activities of the day, one may ask oneself daily, "Am I growing in goodness? Am I pursuing the right, the true, and the beautiful?" Elsewhere, Marcus recommends the following practice: In the morning when you rise unwillingly from your bed, let this thought be present: I am rising to the work of a human being. Why then am I dissatisfied if I am going to do the things for which I exist and for which I was brought into the world? Or have I been made for this, to lie under the covers and keep myself warm? These exhortations are practice-oriented. Marcus never loses sight of the fundamental fact of the precariousness and brevity of human life. So, his recurrent refrain is to live with a sense of utmost urgency: "This is the mark of perfection of character—to spend each day as if it were your last, without frenzy, laziness, or any pretending". Marcus Aurelius constantly asks himself: 'Are my guiding principles healthy and robust? On this hangs everything.' Elsewhere, he reminds us: You could leave life right now. Let that determine what you do and say and think.

Wisdom, in all these forms, mainly requires understanding the difference between good, bad, and indifferent things. Virtue is good and vice is bad, but everything else is indifferent. Indeed, as we've seen, the Stoics followed the Cynics in maintaining the hard line that virtue is the only true good. However, Zeno went on to distinguish between indifferent things that are "preferred," "dispreferred," or completely indifferent.

Put crudely, external things do have some value, but they're not worth getting upset over—it's a different kind of value. One way Stoics explained this was by saying that if we could put virtue on one side of a set of scales, it wouldn't matter how many gold coins or other indifferent things piled up on the opposing side—it should never tip the balance. Nevertheless, some external things are preferable to others, and wisdom consists precisely in our ability to make these sorts of value judgments. Life is preferable to death, wealth is preferable to poverty, health is preferable to sickness, friends are preferable to enemies, and so on.

Moreover, the Stoics' concept of cosmopolitanism becomes evident, challenging the conventional distinctions between different groups, particularly the Greeks and the so-called "barbarians." They viewed the universe as their "polis" or city, fostering a sense of being "cosmopolitan." This ancient wisdom advocates for the interconnectedness of individuals with the larger world, promoting universal harmony and a shared responsibility toward the global community. Marcus Aurelius, while not explicitly using the term "cosmopolitan," identifies himself as a citizen not only of Rome but also as a citizen of the world, transcending narrow nationalistic affiliations.

Marcus Aurelius warns against the allure of power and advises accepting leadership only when absolutely necessary, considering it as a duty rather than a coveted position. He advocates for leaders who reluctantly assume authority, propelled by necessity and driven by the responsibility to prevent inferior rule. This stands in stark contrast to contemporary leaders who often seek power for personal gain and self-aggrandizement. The emperor's memorable passage from the Meditations relinquishes the trappings of power, emphasizing the importance of simplicity, virtue, and adherence to philosophical principles. He implores individuals to strive for goodness, remain humble, uphold justice, and foster mutual care, recognizing life's brevity and the significance of cultivating a virtuous character for the collective welfare.

Ethics and Power

Ethics and power have long been intertwined in the discourse of philosophy and governance. Stoic philosophy, including the teachings of Marcus Aurelius, provides insights into the relationship between ethics and the responsible exercise of power. Stoicism emphasizes that true power lies not in external control or dominance but in mastering one's inner self and aligning actions with virtue and moral principles. Marcus Aurelius, as a Stoic emperor, advocated for a leadership style grounded in ethical values, stressing the importance of using power with wisdom, fairness, and benevolence.

Chapter 13: Human Nature Understanding the Self Connecting with Others

When it comes to wellbeing, other people matter. Evidence shows that connecting with others and forming good relationships – with family, friends and the wider community – are important for mental wellbeing.

Building stronger, broader social connections in your life can increase your feelings of happiness and self-worth.

Many of us would like to spend more time with people who are important to us. Sometimes, having a busy life can make this difficult.

But evidence shows that our relationships affect both our physical health and mental wellbeing. Mental wellbeing means feeling good – about ourselves and the world around us – and functioning well.

Nurturing our relationships can help us feel happier and more secure, and can give us a greater sense of purpose. That makes investing in relationships one of the five evidence-based steps we can all take to improve our mental wellbeing.

Human nature, a fundamental theme in Stoic philosophy, embodies the belief that individuals possess an innate capacity for reason and virtue. Stoics view human beings as rational creatures capable of exercising control over their thoughts, actions, and emotions. Marcus Aurelius, influenced by Stoic principles, emphasized the significance of human rationality as a tool for understanding the world and navigating life's challenges. He believed that embracing reason enables individuals to cultivate virtue, exercise moral judgment, and lead a life aligned with nature's principles.

Stoicism contends that humans are interconnected with the universe and are integral parts of a larger cosmic order. This philosophy emphasizes the harmony between the individual and the natural world. Stoics perceive humanity as a microcosm of the macrocosm, illustrating that individuals are interconnected with the universal order and share a collective responsibility toward maintaining cosmic harmony. Marcus Aurelius often reflected on this interconnectedness, encouraging individuals to recognize their place within the broader context of the universe and to act in accordance with its rational principles. Stoicism's view of human nature revolves around the acceptance of life's transience and the impermanence of existence. Stoics, including Marcus Aurelius, advocated for an acceptance of the cyclical nature of life and its inevitable changes. They believed in adapting to the ebb and flow of life, recognizing that human existence is fleeting and subject to constant flux. This perspective encouraged individuals to develop resilience, maintain an inner tranquility, and focus on what lies within their control while accepting what is beyond it.

Whenever anything goes wrong in our life, we naturally seek an explanation. To not find some cause for why our plans went awry, or why we faced sudden resistance to our ideas, would be deeply disturbing to us and intensify our pain.

The first step toward becoming rational is to understand our fundamental irrationality. There are two factors that should render this more palatable to our egos: nobody is exempt from the irresistible effect of emotions on the mind, not even the wisest among us; and to some extent irrationality is a function of the structure of our brains and is wired into our very nature by the way we process emotions. Being irrational is almost beyond our control.

Below the conscious level, emotions are constantly influencing our decisions and mental processes. The need for pleasure and the need to stay away from suffering are the most prevalent emotions of all. This need usually always occupies our minds, and we simply turn away from concepts that make us uncomfortable or painful. When in reality we are clinging to beliefs that relieve stress, stroke our egos, and give us a sense of superiority, we pretend we are seeking the truth or being realistic. All of our mental biases stem from this pleasure principle in thought.

If you believe that you are somehow immune to any of the following biases, it is simply an example of the pleasure principle in action. Instead, it is best to search and see how they continually operate inside you, as well as learn how to identify such irrationality in others.

Chapter 14: Death and Impermanence Acceptance of Mortality

Two fundamental aspects of the human experience that influence how we view life are death and impermanence. Many philosophical and spiritual systems have considered the impermanence of existence and the certainty of death throughout history, including stoicism. For example, stoicism urges people to accept life's fleeting character and acknowledge that everything in the material world is ephemeral. In order to find peace and acceptance, this ideology places a strong emphasis on realizing that everything is temporary.

Death, which is frequently seen as the one thing that is guaranteed, makes one consider the legacy they leave behind. The realization that one will eventually die may be a source of inspiration for personal development, inspiring people to live meaningful lives and make a good difference in the world and other people. Being aware of life's impermanence may bring comfort, inspiring people to welcome change and overcome obstacles with fortitude since it emphasizes how important it is to savor each moment. In pursuit of quality care, he so moves from hospital to hospital and from doctor to doctor until finally he runs out of money. But he doesn't stop there. He obtains a loan and proceeds with a costly medical procedure. However, that doesn't work either. And after that, he passes very quickly!

This is the narrative of nearly every human being on the planet, not just one individual. For us, growing older truly serves as a warning that death is imminent. As you age, you become vulnerable to several illnesses. This is meant to jolt you and awaken you to the fact that death is inevitable. Not too far away. Illness awakens you from slumber by forcing you to confront it. It appears to compel you to get up if you are awake. And it's to make you walk if you've already stood up. Being sick serves as a wake-up call that your time to die is almost here.

You always have to face the realities of old age and its accompanying challenges in order to begin preparing for your impending mortality before it really happens. This allows you to think carefully about what might be in store for you in the hereafter and make plans for the remainder of your time here on Earth. However, the majority of people actually gain very little from these kinds of experiences. While illness and old age are warning signs or heralds of impending death, people only consider getting better when these things happen!

Moreover, the acceptance of mortality serves as a catalyst for self-reflection and living a more meaningful existence. Recognizing life's impermanence prompts individuals to ponder the brevity of their time on Earth and contemplate the legacy they wish to leave behind.

This contemplation often leads to a reevaluation of personal values, fostering a deeper appreciation for life and encouraging individuals to prioritize experiences, relationships, and pursuits that align with their authentic selves.

Reflections on Life and Death

Humans desire to live forever, but we are usually compelled to depart this world against our choice within a hundred years or less at the latest. The two fundamental experiences that all people go through are the experiences of life and death. If you give these two events some real thought, you will undoubtedly come to the astounding conclusion that we were put here for an examination rather than as a reward for anything. We believe and feel that we are free in this world.

We have been given this freedom so as that it can be ascertained who among us has used this freedom properly and led a principled life, and who has not done so. If you think about that seriously, you will realize that death is the moment of our having to appear before God. We are actually eternal beings, but, as mentioned earlier, our lives are divided into two periods: the pre-death and post-death periods. The former period is for the purpose of being tested, while the latter period is when we will be rewarded or punished, as the case might be, according to the record of our deeds in the pre-death phase of our lives.

We now recognize ourselves as sentient, conscious entities. And when we pass away, we will be sent to the hereafter while we are still alive and cognizant. That amazing day is coming for all of us, sooner or later. It would be the most serious moment of my life. We shall always be the same creatures that we were before death, yet everything that we had while here on Earth will be taken from us forever. We will have left behind for good the world where we had spent the short pre-death period of our lives. In front of us another world will stretch, where we will have to live for eternity. A truly wise man is he who prepares himself adequately for this day.

Death, however, is a bold rebuttal of this worldview. Everyone has to die one day, and so all the worldly wealth you have accumulated will one day be snatched from you.

You will have to give up the small universe you have devoted all of your time, effort, and resources to creating forever. You'll be directed toward

If you did not sufficiently prepare for such a world while in this world, you will find yourself in one in which you have nothing at all. Upon birth, all individuals quickly adopt the same worldview as others in their immediate vicinity.

He becomes involved in a variety of materialistically driven activities, just like them. This has led to the integration of materialistic thought into the ongoing narrative of human history.

This sort of thinking has become such an integral part of cultural traditions that it seems almost impossible for anyone to be able to think free from it. We must work on developing ourselves in such a way that in the eternal life that will unfold after death we will be considered to be successful.

Chapter 15: Conclusions and Legacy of Marcus Aurelius

Renowned as the final of Rome's "Five Good Emperors," Marcus Aurelius left behind a lasting legacy that extended beyond his time as an emperor. His philosophical work "Meditations," which he wrote as a collection of his own personal reflections rather than a formal treatise, has had a profound impact on Stoic philosophy and is still read and studied by many people today.

Aurelius's "Meditations" is a timeless treasure trove of knowledge, including counsel on living a moral life as well as deep insights into the human condition. His philosophical observations on acceptance, inner peace, ethics, and resiliency have endured since antiquity, speaking to readers who are looking for comfort, insight, and direction in overcoming the challenges of life.

Marcus Aurelius is admired for his leadership style, which is marked by a dedication to justice, fairness, and the wellbeing of his people, in addition to his philosophical achievements. He was a living example of the Stoic values that he advocated in his works, which emphasized the value of moral rectitude, self-control, and compassion in leadership. His reign was characterized by initiatives to advance justice and equity in Roman society, which had a long-lasting effect on the fundamentals of government and leadership.

Aurelius's legacy extends beyond philosophy and governance. His life serves as a testament to the integration of philosophical principles into daily life, showcasing the profound impact that personal introspection and philosophical contemplation can have on shaping an individual's character and actions. His enduring influence lies not only in the pages of his written reflections but also in the embodiment of Stoic virtues that continue to inspire seekers of wisdom and seekers of a meaningful, purpose-driven life.

The Impact of Meditations Over Time, Meditation as an alternative mind-body therapy

It is a popular intervention to improve mental and physical health. People have been meditating for thousands of years, often as part of a spiritual practice. But in more recent years, meditation has become a popular way to help people manage their stress and improve their overall well-being- and a wealth of research shows it's effective. Psychologists have found that meditation changes our brain and biology in positive ways, improving mental and physical health. There is discussion of how meditation affects human physiology, or physical health, including heart rate, blood pressure, metabolism, brain activity, and skin resistance. Discussions are also held regarding the effects of meditation on human mental health, including relaxation, systematic desensitization, the release of repressed memory, perception, memory, stress, depression, anxiety, sleep disturbance, and de-stressing. Lastly, important conceptual difficulties are covered that require careful consideration by scholars in this field for upcoming studies.

Meditation is a mental practice where an individual exercises their mind to have a state of focus, to train attention, and to create self-awareness. The goals of meditation are to attain a state of consciousness that is mentally clear and emotionally calm. Meditation practices mainly changes functions through autonomous nervous system, which links brain and body.

With meditation, the physiology undergoes a change, and every cell in the body is filled with more prana (energy). These results in joy, peace, enthusiasm as the level of prana in the body increases. On a physical level, meditation:

Reduces hypertension Decreases blood lactate levels, lessening panic episodes Reduces pain associated with tension, including headaches, stomach ulcers, sleeplessness, and issues with muscles and joints. Boosts serotonin synthesis, which elevates mood and behavior Boosts the immune system and enhances sleep quality

The Legacy of Marcus Aurelius Today

The influence of Marcus Aurelius is still felt today in a variety of fields, including leadership, philosophy, personal growth, and mindfulness. His "Meditations," written as a private journal of stoic philosophy, remain a pillar of knowledge for people looking for direction in overcoming obstacles in life. Within a contemporary setting, Aurelius's observations on fortitude, tolerance, and moral behavior provide insightful viewpoints that cut over time and cultural barriers.

The ideas explained by Marcus Aurelius have found application in a number of fields, like as self-improvement, leadership, and psychiatry. His focus on the value of self-awareness and the strength of perception strikes a deep chord with modern mindfulness and cognitive-behavioral therapies. Many self-help philosophies and modern stoicism incorporate his ideas on accepting external occurrences that are beyond one's control and on understanding and managing one's thinking.

The significant influence of Marcus Aurelius can be seen in discussions of morality and ethics in the modern world. His support of moral behavior, giving ethical behavior first priority, and aiming for personal greatness offers a philosophical basis for ethical issues in a variety of contexts, such as politics, business ethics, and personal growth. His lasting influence emphasizes the eternal value of moral values and decency in the complicated and fast-paced world of today.

Many individuals seek solace in Stoicism's teachings, especially during times of uncertainty, stress, and rapid change.

Nowadays, stoicism is more well-liked as a useful ideology for controlling emotions, building mental toughness, and overcoming hardship. Its focus on differentiating between things that are under one's control and those that are not has proven very helpful in overcoming obstacles in daily life. This school of thought promotes emotional resilience and a sense of agency by encouraging people to pay attention to how they react to situations rather than dwelling on external factors.

The appeal of stoicism in the modern world has spread beyond matters of personal wellbeing and into the domains of business, leadership, and personal growth. Many leaders incorporate stoic ideas into their leadership philosophies as a source of inspiration. The stoic emphasis on morality, humility, and the quest of perfection offers leaders looking to strike a balance between ambition and moral integrity a model. Its emphasis on moral qualities like justice, integrity, and fortitude acts as a compass for people navigating the intricacies of today's problems.

With its focus on morality and integrity, stoic ethics and morality provide insightful analysis and useful direction in today's world. The four cardinal qualities of wisdom, courage, justice, and temperance are the foundation of virtuous character that the Stoics promoted. They also encouraged living in harmony with nature. These virtues are still relevant in today's world, offering a moral compass to those looking for moral guidance in both their personal and professional life.

Chapter 16: The Role of Nature in Stoicism

Stoic philosophy is deeply rooted in nature, which functions as a compass for comprehending the universe and our place in it. Stoics held that one should live in harmony with the natural world, directing one's thoughts and deeds in accordance with the universe's inherent order. The fundamental tenet of this philosophy is that people should make an effort to understand and embrace the reasonable, consistent rules that govern nature.

Stoicism emphasizes the interdependence of all things in the universe and the interwoven web of existence. The realization that people are a component of a bigger, interconnected system is the foundation of the Stoic concept of cosmopolitanism, or seeing oneself as a citizen of the world. This viewpoint urges people to broaden their empathy, compassion, and care beyond their own interests to include the welfare of all people.

The Stoics also discovered knowledge and comfort in studying nature. They looked to nature as a source of wisdom, drawing philosophical conclusions from contemplating its rules, cycles, and patterns. Stoics held that people may learn more about virtue, knowledge, and the laws guiding human existence by examining the natural world. In modern Stoic practices, this respect for nature and its lessons is still present, encouraging mindfulness, regard for the natural world, and a sense of oneness.

Marcus Aurelius' View of Nature and Living in Accordance with Nature

The philosophical inquiry into the correlation between living a good life and being a good person finds resonance across various virtue ethicists. They all concur that a good life is intrinsically linked to being a good person. This commonality echoes through the tenets of Confucianism, Aristotelian ethics, and Stoicism. While Confucianism emphasizes benevolence, righteousness, propriety, and placing paramount importance on harmony, Aristotelian ethics emphasizes moderation, courage, and justice. On the other hand, Stoicism, advocating for living in harmony with nature, emphasizes the cultivation of wisdom, moderation, courage, and the pursuit of what's under one's control.

Stoicism's approach to a good life underscores living in harmony with nature and others. It emphasizes focusing on what's under one's control, which involves an individual's power of choice, desires, and actions. The Stoic view contends that the only good for an individual is virtue and highlights the importance of responding well to impressions by using reason. Stoics believe that the Sage, someone who possesses knowledge and responds well to impressions, lives in complete harmony with nature. However, the practicality of achieving such a state for most individuals remains an ongoing process, whereby they strive to be "Progressors" in alignment with Stoic ideals.

The Stoic notion of cosmopolitanism emphasizes the importance of being a global citizen. It includes realizing oneself in relation to all of humanity and the natural world, as well as expanding circles of affinity. In his Meditations, Marcus Aurelius demonstrates a profound comprehension of human nature. He emphasizes the importance of accepting humanity's innate connectedness in spite of personal shortcomings or transgressions.

Marcus argues that ignorance is the root of all wrongdoing and that we should not let other people's actions to hurt us because there is nothing that is truly beyond our control. Another Stoic philosopher, Epictetus, supports this idea by making a distinction between what is under our control and what is not, advocating freedom as the administration of what is under our control.

The Stoic system, spanning physics, logic, and ethics, attempts to unravel the nature of reality, knowledge, and the good life. Stoic physics perceives everything as material and governed by a passive and active principle, with reason (logos) permeating the cosmos and imparting order. The logical aspect of Stoicism involves understanding how impressions shape our beliefs and the significance of responding to true impressions. The pinnacle of Stoic ethics is living in agreement with nature, where virtue equals wisdom, and the good life is grounded in responding well to what's under one's control. The Stoic emphasis on logic, ethics, and cosmopolitanism offers profound insights into navigating life's complexities in harmony with oneself, others, and the natural order.

The fundamental tenet of the stoic outlook on morality and life is that real happiness can only be obtained by accepting what is under our control and living in harmony with the natural world. As a philosophy, stoicism places a strong emphasis on developing reason, accepting life as it happens, and realizing one has free will. It emphasizes how crucial it is to concentrate on one's inner states, cultivate qualities like courage, wisdom, moderation, and justice, and recognize that one's environment is frequently outside of one's control. Stoics support a way of living in which people follow reason, acknowledge that things happen temporarily, and put all of their attention into growing morally within.

The philosophical system of stoicism likewise emphasizes the interdependence of the cosmos and humans. A model of virtue, the Stoic Sage is described as existing in perfect harmony with the natural world.

For Stoics, this ideal is an aspirational goal, even though it is unachievable for most. It implies that people can live peaceful and happy lives by following the path of virtue and being in harmony with the natural world. The Stoic emphasis on cosmopolitanism, or seeing oneself as a global citizen, encourages collaboration and acknowledges the innate bonds that unite all people, which serves to further emphasize the interdependence of humans and the larger universe.

Marcus Aurelius had a deep understanding of nature, perceiving it as a harmonious interaction of elements guided by purpose and reason. 'Meditations' is a collection of his writings that frequently express his respect for nature. Aurelius marveled by the universe's beauty and recognized its innate order and interdependence. He held the fundamental Stoic belief that everything in the universe is interrelated and works harmoniously because of a rational design.

Marcus Aurelius believed that nature was more than just the physical universe; rather, it was an expression of "logos," or universal reason. He observed that everything was infused with this divine reason, which dictated the world's order. Similar to the teachings of the Stoics, this concept emphasized that rational rules govern the world and that people should endeavor to live in harmony with this universal order. Aurelius frequently advocated embracing nature's unchangeable principles, letting go of personal preferences, and realizing that all experiences—both good and bad—are a part of this larger, more purposeful plan.

Chapter 17: Overcoming External Challenges

A major idea of stoicism is overcoming external obstacles, which entails developing resilience and preserving inner peace in the face of uncontrollable difficulties. Stoics support a way of thinking that distinguishes between things that are under our control and those that are not. People can overcome obstacles with composure if they only concentrate on their own ideas, deeds, and reactions and accept that other events are mostly beyond their control.

According to stoicism, the secret to conquering outside obstacles is to manage our emotions and reactions to them rather than trying to control the events themselves, which are frequently out of our control. Through the development of inner virtues, resilience, and self-control, people can overcome external circumstances and maintain inner peace and well-being while navigating challenges with courage and knowledge.

We can also put this concept into practice by learning to let go of things that are beyond of our control. This could entail letting go of the need to dictate to others how things should happen or the want to control them. Furthermore, embracing what cannot be changed is closely related to the concept of resilience. When people accept and overcome difficult circumstances and barriers, they become more resilient and are better equipped to deal with stress in the future. In today's fast-paced world, where stress and struggle are inevitable, this is vital.

Stoicism in the Face of External Adversity

Philosophers such as Marcus Aurelius and Epictetus, who personified stoicism, advocated for inner strength and resilience in the face of external hardships. Stoicism's central idea is to discern between the things that are and are not under our control. The theory emphasizes accepting that we have no control over outside events and instead concentrating on our own attitudes, judgments, and behaviors. It encourages handling difficulties with poise, reason, and a morally-driven attitude as opposed to letting feelings get in the way.

In his 'Meditations,' Marcus Aurelius stressed the need of remaining calm in the face of difficulty. He exhorted people to view the world objectively and distance themselves from the emotional upheaval brought on by uncontrollable situations. This stoic method embraces that difficulties are unavoidable parts of life and guides emotions with reason rather than encouraging them to be repressed. Stoicism teaches people to adapt and survive by accepting that trials are inevitable and to see them as chances for personal development.

Stoicism's emphasis on building an inner fortress of virtue, marked by moral strength and emotional stability, accounts for its perseverance in the face of outside adversity. The concept encourages people to concentrate on their moral behavior, stressing virtues like self-control, patience, and a reasonable acceptance of life's uncertainty. Stoicism emphasizes the value of remaining collected and peaceful no matter what is going on around you. It also helps you develop mental toughness and a sense of empowerment even in the most difficult circumstances.

Adversities, according to the Stoics, offer a chance to show how committed one is to virtue. Stoics promoted viewing adversity as a chance for moral development and resilience rather than letting it weaken one's moral compass. They held that hardship was an opportunity to demonstrate one's dedication to virtues like temperance, patience, and compassion, strengthening one's moral character and inner fortitude. Retaining virtue under trying conditions is essential to stoic thought. People can maintain their inner virtues and behave with knowledge, fairness, and courage even when faced with difficult circumstances by emphasizing moral perfection and realizing that external events are beyond their control.

This approach enables individuals to uphold their integrity and ethical values, fostering resilience and fortitude amidst life's trials.

Chapter 18: The Search for Wisdom Philosophy as a Way of Life

Wisdom is something we all have reason to care about. Indeed, many ancient and contemporary moral philosophers, whose goal is to seek well-reasoned answers to questions about how we ought to live, have concluded that wisdom is a central component of a well lived life. This has led them to explore questions like: Are there different kinds of wisdom? What kind of a state is wisdom? Is wisdom a kind of knowledge or understanding, or is it a skill or a complex set of dispositions? How does wisdom relate to other virtues (excellent traits)? What kind(s) of reasoning, if any, do wise people engage in to decide what to do? What role do emotions and knowledge play in wisdom?

"Philosophy as a Way of Life" summarizes the Stoic view that philosophical ideas are useful guidance for wisdom, leading a happy and moral life rather than just cerebral exercises. Marcus Aurelius and Epictetus are two great examples of stoicism, which emphasizes the practical application of philosophical principles to overcome obstacles in life rather than only knowing things theoretically. It places a strong emphasis on turning philosophical ideas into practical applications that shape behavior and character.

For Stoics, philosophy is a constant practice rather than a theoretical pursuit. It involves actively cultivating virtues like wisdom, courage, justice, and temperance in everyday life. This entails incorporating philosophical precepts into daily actions, interactions, and decisions, aligning one's thoughts and behaviors with reason and moral principles.

An integral part of philosophy as a lifestyle is introspection and self-reflection. The value of pondering on one's deeds, thoughts, and emotions is emphasized by stoicism.

The goal of this introspective process is to recognize and address one's own shortcomings in order to get oneself closer to virtue and reason. People can live stoically by taking regular inventory of themselves and making an effort to improve.

Philosophy is a conversion, a transformation of one's way of being and living, and a quest for wisdom." 2. It is the practice of what Hadot calls "spiritual exercises" that brings about self-transformation and makes philosophy a way of life.

For the Greeks and Romans, doing philosophy meant choosing a school and adopting their way of life. It involved what today would be called a religious conversion. "The philosophical school …demands from the individual a total change of lifestyle, a conversion of one's entire being, and…a…desire to be and live in a certain way." Each school had their own set of spiritual exercises that corresponded to their respective ideals of wisdom.

The students practiced reading, writing, research, and dialogue—activities that are still commonly associated with academic study. However, they also used activities that we associate with spiritual or religious institutions, such as self-control drills, therapy to subdue emotions, introspection, meditation, and learning the school's tenets by heart.

In 529 AD the Christian Emperor, Justinian, closed the Athenian Academy, a neo-Platonic school, and brought to an end the teaching of classical philosophy in the West.

Now, philosophy was relegated to serving as theology's handmaiden, providing philosophical concepts and language to uphold the church's dogmas, and Christianity was seen as the exclusive way of living.

Philosophy's spiritual practices were incorporated into Christian spirituality.

According to Hadot, the exercises performed by Thomas à Kempis and Saint Ignatius of Loyola are only Christian adaptations of these antiquated customs. Rather than being wise, spiritual practice was shaped by imitating Christ. Paul said, "I will destroy the wisdom of the wise..." While the Greeks seek wisdom, we preach the crucified Christ.

For Hadot, the poverty of modern philosophy is the consequence of the abandonment of spiritual exercises. With the waning of Christianity and the rise of secularism, there has been a re-emergence of philosophy understood as a way of life.

The Stoics did not seek to control or moderate the passions, rather they sought their elimination. For them, the good life is a life without passion. The Stoic sage is apatheia, from the Greek meaning without feeling.

The Stoic urges us not to give importance to external things. When we attach ourselves to what is not under our control we set ourselves up for upset and grief. Love, for instance, brings with it fear of losing it, anger when it is threatened, envy if someone else has it, and grief over its loss. For the Stoics, the passions are the source of all our sorrow.

It is undeniably untrue that a Stoic believes in total self-sufficiency, but there is merit to an individual who is not possessed by the world's glitter. Positively speaking, the Stoic is defined as "a self-commanding person—someone who, simply by refusing to submit to the forces of fate, is truly free—rather than being the slave of fortune." She gives herself orders on everything that's necessary to live a good life. The wise person is the only one who is truly free in a society where most people cherish things like money that seem to bring power but actually offer slavery.

"…man lives in the world without perceiving the world." 18. Pierre Hadot

Only until we set ourselves free from the past and the future can we truly be in the present. The way we experience time needs to be completely different from our daily lives, when we constantly oscillate between regret and worry, expectation and remembrance, and ultimately lose sight of the now. "For the ancients, "separating oneself from the future and past" in order to "delimit the present instant" was a key component of exercises that required focusing one's mind on the present moment, and doing so was closely associated with changing one's perspective on the world.

Learning and Growing Through Stoic Teachings

At its core, Stoic philosophy encourages individuals to embrace life as a journey of learning and self-improvement. Central to this approach is the notion of applying reason and cultivating moral excellence as a means of attaining inner tranquility and resilience in the face of adversities.

Making the distinction between what is within and outside of our control is one of the core tenets of stoicism. Stoicism provides a useful method for personal development by emphasizing our ideas, decisions, and attitudes—the things we can control. It exhorts people to focus on cultivating virtues that are the cornerstone of a fulfilling and moral life, such as courage, wisdom, justice, and self-discipline.

The tenets of stoicism promote lifelong learning from both positive and unpleasant situations. Setbacks do not demoralize stoics; rather, they present chances for personal development. Adversities are viewed as opportunities to practice fortitude, tenacity, and the ability to grow from adversity. By logically dissecting these events, people acquire understanding that advances their own growth.

Moreover, self-awareness and introspection are valued aspects of stoicism. People can find areas for growth and become more closely aligned with Stoic ideas by routinely analyzing their thoughts, feelings, and behaviors. Self-reflection facilitates a deeper understanding of oneself and the pursuit of personal improvement, which in turn supports continuous learning and growth along the Stoic path.

As a way of living, stoicism provides an organized framework that converts its virtues into useful suggestions for improving oneself. Stoic philosophy places a strong emphasis on what a person can control. This exercise encourages a change in perspective that places more emphasis on accepting accountability for one's decisions and responses to outside events.

Stoicism encourages people to focus their emphasis on what is within their sphere of influence and emphasizes the importance of making wise decisions rather than obsessing on the circumstances. This promotes a sense of agency and empowerment.

Chapter 19: Embracing Change and Impermanence

Living requires adjusting to change. Accepting that change is inevitable and that everything in life is transient can be excruciatingly unpleasant. Many of us fiercely fight the inevitable changes in our bodies, minds, and emotions that come with aging, clinging to ideals of who we think we are or were. We can also discover that we are firmly rooted in a pervasive denial that those around us are also evolving. We have to acknowledge that all material objects are transient in addition to being vulnerable to change.

Take a moment to look around you – notice the delicate temporary nature to all things in their material forms. Rather than allowing this recognition of impermanence to instill fear in your heart, consider the potential for increasing mindful awareness, deepening and cherishing relationships, and discovering yourself amidst change. As soon as it becomes clear that each passing moment is a gift that you can choose to connect with or not, your perspective on how you live your life may begin to shift.

Think about how misery results from clinging. Acknowledging and embracing transience does not necessitate holding onto what we believe to be ours - intelligence, beauty, wealth, possessions, or romantic relationships. These items were never really "ours" in the first place. Accepting impermanence entails being attentive of and accepting this basic reality. Fear may first surface when we let go of the vice-like hold we frequently have over these attachments, but in the end, the process of letting go can release us from needless suffering.

It can be particularly difficult to let go of people, objects, or symbols that we have been very attached to and internalized as being an integral part of who we really are. Imagine the suffering that someone would have if they spent their entire life creating and loving their family and then watched them all go.

Or consider the suffering of devoting years of one's life to following a dream or goal that you truly love, only to have it snatched away from you or never reach. Not the loss itself, but the holding on is what causes the anguish.

This is not to say that there is no potential for tragic losses and transformations. The majority of us have felt the intense emotional suffering that comes with losing a piece of our identity or our desire to be, ending a relationship we believed would continue "forever," or losing sight of a dream we once had. One can connect to the pain that results from these kinds of losses in a different way. Pain is unavoidable, just as change is; the choice to suffer is not.

The philosophy of stoicism offers a profound viewpoint on accepting change and realizing that life is temporary. Fundamentally, stoicism urges people to acknowledge that life is fleeting. The philosophy places a strong emphasis on the idea that change is a necessary part of life and that rejecting it can be painful. Stoics, on the other hand, support accepting change, realizing that it is out of our control, and concentrating our energy on how we react to these changes.

The idea of impermanence, or the idea that everything in life is transitory, is frequently emphasized in stoic teachings. Through acknowledging the transient essence of everything, stoicism encourages people to develop a detached mindset from material belongings and outside events. This detachment encourages people to value their inner values and personal development over the transient nature of situations or objects outside of themselves, rather than implying apathy or indifference.

Furthermore, stoicism promotes living in the now and avoiding attachment to the past or the future. The ideology teaches people to enjoy the present without undue attachment or aversion, seeing that dwelling on the past or worrying about the future prevents people from truly experiencing and living in the now.

The Stoic Approach to Change

The foundation of the stoic approach to change is the conviction that change is an unavoidable aspect of life and that fighting it will only cause internal strife. Stoicism encourages people to accept change by concentrating on their behaviors and attitudes, which they can control, as opposed to obsessing over uncontrollably occurring external events. The Stoics stressed that although we are not always in control of the situations or things that happen in our lives, we are in charge of how we respond to and interpret them.

Understanding the nature of impermanence is central to the Stoic philosophy. According to stoic philosophy, nothing in life is permanent and everything is fleeting. This knowledge encourages people to put internal values and personal development ahead of attachments to transient material things or circumstances. Stoicism helps people discover stability inside themselves by acknowledging the transience of outside circumstances, which empowers them to handle change with poise and perseverance.

Stoicism's idea of impermanence and accepting change fearlessly are similar. Stoics place a strong emphasis on changing one's perspective to acknowledge that life is full of unpredictable changes. People who practice stoicism can cultivate a sense of peace and mental toughness by removing oneself from an excessive emotional attachment to fleeting circumstances by acknowledging their impermanence.

Additionally, stoicism promotes mindfulness training and an emphasis on the here and now. By engaging in mindfulness practices, people can better control their reactions by becoming more aware of their thoughts and feelings. Rather of letting their emotions control them through impulsive or reactive reactions to outside stimuli, stoics think that emotions can be used as signals to implement thoughtful and helpful coping mechanisms.

A framework for embracing change flexibly and truthfully is provided by stoicism. People can discover a route to inner freedom and authenticity by accepting impermanence and letting go of the false self—the delusions and attachments that frequently cause misery. According to stoicism, one can respond to life's ups and downs with resilience, adaptability, and a greater sense of self-awareness and authenticity by practicing acceptance of change without fear.

Chapter 20: The Stoic Community and Legacy

The focus placed by the Stoic philosophy on morality, virtue, and perseverance in the face of hardship has cultivated a thriving global society and continues to have an impact on contemporary thought. Stoicism's practical outlook on life, which provides insightful observations that are relevant to today's issues, is what has left an enduring legacy. Online and in-person stoic communities have grown, uniting people looking for advice on how to apply stoic ideas to the challenges of everyday life.

Social media groups, internet forums, and resource sharing are ways that stoic practitioners interact, converse, and assist one another in putting stoic teachings into practice. These groups offer a forum for people to debate how to apply stoic practices to their contemporary lives, ask questions, and study the tenets of stoicism. Moreover, people from a variety of backgrounds attend the yearly Stoic Week events and Stoicon conferences, which feature talks, workshops, and debates about the real-world applications of stoicism.

The influence of stoicism is felt not just in local social circles but also in larger cultural contexts. Numerous domains, including psychology, self-help, leadership, and ethics, have been impacted by its principles. Numerous well-known people have adopted stoic philosophy, including politicians, businesspeople, and athletes. They see its benefits in developing mental clarity, emotional fortitude, and tenacity in the face of adversity. The writings of stoic philosophers such as Seneca, Epictetus, and Marcus Aurelius are still read and studied today because they offer eternal knowledge and direction to people looking for stability, meaning, and purpose in a constantly changing world.

The philosophical reflections of Socrates and Plato serve as the foundation for stoicism, which was further developed by Chrysippus and Zeno of Citium. Rome saw a steady rise in the popularity of this philosophy, thanks in large part to the work of notable individuals like Cicero and Seneca the Younger. One fascinating feature of stoicism is how inclusive it is; its adherents come from a variety of backgrounds, including emperor Marcus Aurelius and slave Epictetus. This diversity is a reflection of the primary message of stoicism, which emphasizes the pursuit of virtue and knowledge as goals that are available to everyone due to their shared ability for reason, regardless of their exterior circumstances.

One feature of Stoic philosophy is embodied in the modern notion of a stoic as someone who is immune to the emotional upheaval and anguish that befall others. This perception, nevertheless, needs to be understood in the context of a broader all-encompassing life philosophy.

Stoicism completely rejected the use of passions to judge what is right or wrong, relying on Plato's idea that human passions and appetites may be controlled by reason. It promoted the idea that the only thing fit to judge the worth or badness of things pursued is reason, independent of desire.

Understanding that ultimate goodness rests in wisdom and virtue, the wise Stoic forgoes longing for the satisfaction of bodily wants, identifying instead with reason.

One of stoicism's lasting contributions is its conviction that all people are capable of reason. This belief went beyond the narrow Greek definition of equal citizenship and instead promoted a deep sense of equality. Seneca stressed that the sensible person should value the society of rational beings more than any specific group that is predetermined by birth. In a same vein, Marcus Aurelius emphasized the concept of common reason as something that transcends personal identities and promotes a sense of citizenship among everyone. Stoics' advocacy of a universal moral code, which served as a framework to oppose ethical relativism, was based on their conviction that all people are capable of reason.

Marcus Aurelius and the Stoic Community of His Time

The philosophy of the Roman Emperor Marcus Aurelius can be found in a collection of personal writings known as the *Meditations*. These reflect the influence of Stoicism and, in particular, the philosophy of Epictetus, the Stoic. The *Meditations* may be read as a series of practical philosophical exercises, following Epictetus' three topics of study, designed to digest and put into practice philosophical theory. Central to these exercises is a concern with the analysis of one's judgements and a desire to cultivate a "cosmic perspective."

While serving as emperor, Marcus Aurelius engaged with the Stoic community through correspondence and discussions with other prominent Stoic thinkers of his time. His exchanges and collaborations with fellow Stoics, such as Claudius Severus, reflected his dedication to philosophical discourse and shared Stoic principles. This active participation and association with Stoic philosophers not only enriched his understanding of Stoicism but also contributed to the integration of Stoic philosophy into his governance, promoting principles of justice, fairness, and rationality within the empire.

The Influence of Stoicism on Later Generations

Marcus Aurelius' philosophical reflections and leadership style reflected the Stoic emphasis on rationality, self-discipline, and the pursuit of moral excellence. His role as both a Stoic practitioner and a political leader demonstrated the interconnectedness between Stoic philosophy and the responsibilities of governance, inspiring a legacy that continues to influence philosophical thought These three areas of training correspond to the three types of philosophical discourse referred to by earlier Stoics; the physical, the ethical, and the logical (see Diogenes Laertius 7.39). For Epictetus, it is not enough merely to discourse about philosophy. The student of philosophy should also engage in practical training designed to digest philosophical principals, transforming them into actions. Only this will enable the apprentice philosopher to transform himself into the Stoic ideal of a wise person or sage (*sophos*). It is to this end that the three *topoi* are directed.

The first topos is devoted to physics and discusses orexis, or desire. Understanding how Nature functions is not sufficient for the philosopher; he also needs to train his wants to only be in harmony with Nature. From the perspective of the Stoic, Nature is an intricately interwoven physical system, associated with God, of which the individual is merely a component. A person who pursues desires without considering how this wider physical system functions will undoubtedly experience frustration and unhappiness. This could be referred to as the practical implication of this idea of Nature. Thus, in order to become a Stoic sage—happy and in harmony with Nature—one must train one's desires in the light of a study of Stoic physical theory.

The second *topos*, concerning impulse (*hormê*), is devoted to ethics. The study of ethical theory is of course valuable in its own right, but, for the Stoic who is training to be a sage, these theories must be translated into ethical actions.

In order to transform the way in which one behaves, it is necessary to train the impulses that shape one's behavior. By so doing the apprentice philosopher will be able not merely to *say* how a sage should act but also to *act* as a sage should act.

Chapter 21: Practical Stoicism in Everyday Life

The tenets of stoicism, developed in antiquity, are still relevant and useful in the complex modern environment. Their lasting significance stems from providing practical direction among the disorder and unpredictability of modern existence. Fundamentally, stoicism promotes concentrating on the things we can control and letting go of the things outside of it. This is an important lesson in the modern world, which is marked by volatility and rapid change. By encouraging people to focus their energies on choices and behaviors that they can control, this idea helps people become resilient and adaptable in the face of adversity.

The Stoic emphasis on distinguishing between what is truly valuable and what is superficial holds particular significance in today's materialistic society. In an era driven by consumerism and external validation, Stoic philosophy urges individuals to prioritize internal virtues over external possessions. It prompts introspection into personal values, emphasizing the cultivation of virtues such as wisdom, courage, justice, and self-discipline as the foundation for a meaningful and fulfilling life.

Furthermore, the negative visualization technique of the Stoics—especially when it comes to thinking about one's own death—is an effective means of obtaining perspective and cultivating thankfulness in modern life. This technique invites people to stop in the middle of the fast-paced world, consider how fleeting life is, and cherish the moment they are in. Through the recognition of transience and the practice of thankfulness, stoicism provides a method to appreciate life's small joys and face hardships with fortitude.

Develop An Internal Locus Of Control

Man is disturbed not by things, but by the views he takes of them." — Epictetus

Much of what happens in life is not within our control. The Stoics recognised this undeniable truth, and focused instead on what they could do.

Born a slave, it would seem that Epictetus had no reason to believe he could control anything. He was permanently crippled from a broken leg given to him by his master. Epictetus would live and die in poverty.

But that wasn't what Epictetus thought. He would say that even while his property and even his body was not within his control, his opinions, desires, and aversions still remained his. That was something that he owned.

It's easy to get frustrated today. We're so used to comfort that even the slightest inconvenience provokes outrage within us. If the internet takes a second longer than it should or if traffic stalls for a minute, the natural instinct is annoyance if not rage.

It isn't any of these breakdowns that are making us unhappy. The unhappiness stems from the emotional response that we have chosen. The onus is on ourselves to ensure that we don't let external events affect our internal state of mind.

Once we internalise that, it becomes clear that we have the power to be happy regardless of our circumstances.

Guard Your Time

"We're tight-fisted with property and money, yet think too little of wasting time, the one thing about which we should all be the toughest misers." — Seneca

The Stoics understood that time is our greatest asset. Unlike any of our material possessions, once lost, time can never be regained. We must therefore strive to waste as little of it as possible.

Those who squander this scarce resource on minutia or entertainment will find that they have nothing to show for it in the end. The habit of procrastination and putting things off will come back to haunt us. Tomorrow isn't guaranteed.

On the other hand, those who give away their time freely to others will also find that they are no better than those who waste it. Most of us allow people and other obligations to impose on our time too easily. We make commitments without giving deep thought to what it entails. Calendars and schedules were meant to help us. We should not become a slave to them.

Regardless of which end of the spectrum we fall into, time is of the essence. We think we have a lot of time, but we really don't.

Don't Outsource Your Happiness

"I have often wondered how it is that every man loves himself more than all the rest of men, but yet sets less value on his own opinions of himself than on the opinions of others." — Marcus Aurelius

Much of what we do stems from our primal need to be liked and accepted by others. Disapproval from our social group had serious repercussions in the past. It would have likely meant exile and eventually death in the wilderness.

That's still true to some extent today. But how much time and effort do we spend trying to win the approval of others? What is it costing us?

We spend money we don't have, to buy fancy things we don't need, in order to impress someone we don't care about. Our choice of career or lifestyle is centred around how others perceive us, rather than what is best for us. We are held hostage and pay a king's ransom every day, with no guarantee that we will ever be free.

The Roman statesman Cato, on the other hand, aimed to live a life unaffected by the opinions of others. He would stroll the streets barefoot and dressed in the most bizarre attire. It was his way of training himself to hate all other kinds of dishonor and to be ashamed only of things that truly deserved it.

He realized Julius Caesar was concentrating too much power and that was the only way he could oppose him. It allowed him to take important decisions without worrying about receiving negative feedback.

He can teach us a lot of things. It would be far better for us to live life independently of other people's perspectives. One should never outsource happiness.

Stay Focused When Confronted With Distractions

"If a person doesn't know to which port they sail, no wind is favourable." — Seneca

Modern-day capitalism has given us an abundance of options.

Whether it's food, travel, or entertainment, we have far more to work with than our predecessors did. Yet, this hasn't clearly benefited us. When presented with so many options, we become paralysed by indecision. We call this the choice paradox. Our brains are overloaded with knowledge since they haven't been able to keep up with the innovations of the modern world. Because choosing is so hard, the default option is to keep things as they are. It's among the main issues we deal with on a daily basis. We never completely commit to a road because there are so many possibilities. Either we delay making a choice or we engage in several tasks concurrently. As a consequence, we never actually advance with anything.

The necessity of deliberate action was emphasized by the Stoics. We have to be careful to live consciously rather than just responding to our environment.

Toss Away Ego And Vanity

"Throw out your conceited opinions, for it is impossible for a person to begin to learn what he thinks he already knows." — Epictetus

One of Epictetus' biggest frustrations as a teacher was how his students claimed to want to be taught, but secretly believed that they knew everything. It's a pain all teachers know and most of us would recognise. At the heart of it is ego and arrogance. The thought is that we've learnt enough and are better than our contemporaries.

Nowhere is such thinking more dangerous than today.

The information of today is not only insufficient for solving the problems of tomorrow but can very well be the obstacle for sharper thinking as well. We are in an age where we're merely one step away from being disrupted in virtually every industry. Even in ancient times Marcus Aurelius has remarked: "the universe is change, life is an opinion".

This is why the most brilliant minds of today spend a good portion of their time reading. They understand that there is always wisdom to be gleaned, whether from the past, present, or future.

Consolidate Your Thoughts In Writing

"No man was ever wise by chance" — Seneca

Of the many things we can do daily, none are as important as looking inward. The act of self-reflection forces us to question ourselves and examine our own assumptions of the world. It's how the answers to some of the world's biggest questions have surfaced.

Keeping a journal remains one of the most effective ways for mindfulness. It boosts creativity, increases gratitude, and serves as therapy all at once. The benefits are numerous. Your thoughts and feelings become clearer in writing than in your mind.

The Stoics understood that well. Whether in a state of peace or conflict, Marcus Aurelius, the most powerful man in the Roman Empire, would obediently take the time to document his observation. It's referred to as meditations in modern times.

Although today's athletes and businesspeople profit greatly from Marcus Aurelius' insights, it is obvious that he benefited most from his own writing and ideas. When anyone else in his situation would have most certainly made a mistake and turned into a despot, the accountability and clarity of thought provided by his journal kept him upright.

Chapter 22: Emotional Resilience and Inner Strength

Stoicism's fundamental tenets of emotional fortitude and interior fortitude mirror the philosophy's emphasis on preserving composure in the face of difficulty. Stoics promote an attitude that views obstacles as chances for personal development rather than as debilitating defeats. This resilience results from realizing that although we have little control over external events, we do have influence over how we react to and interpret them. By recognizing this difference, people can develop an inner resilience that prevents them from being unduly impacted by outside events.

The idea of acceptance lies at the heart of stoic philosophy. Stoics place a strong emphasis on acknowledging that change is inevitable and that existence is temporary. People might find serenity and resilience in the midst of life's uncertainties by accepting the temporary nature of events and realizing that misery frequently results from opposing what cannot be changed. This acceptance permits a change in viewpoint, enabling people to concentrate on what they can control and adjust to uncontrollable situations.

What is an exercise you can give to our readers so they can develop mental toughness?

There are few parameters which we can definitively say, "this is mental toughness" or "this is not mental toughness". There needs to some context because it will look and feel different in different situations. It's the most used and most misunderstood concept in sport. There are a lot of generalized definitions in the literature – most of them have to do with some comparison of yours and your opponent's which makes it only valuable in a relative capacity. I think of it as something we do more than something we have.

Find Meaning – Reflect on and understand what it means to be "tough" in whatever it is you are doing. If we know what it means to be tough in context of what we're doing, we have a goal to pursue and we can start action. The other important reason for meaning is that we all are a little different and so knowing what it is to be tough in a context, to me, really helps outline the thoughts, emotions, and behaviors I need to prepare.

Get Smart – Know your content, inside and out. In sport we call this "Sport IQ", the better understanding we have of how the game works, the easier it is for us to understand what is happening and make decisions. It's also important because focus seems to be a determining factor in mental toughness. We have to know what is important, what isn't important, and when those things change. If we don't know our content well enough to see what context we're in, then it's very difficult to create, maintain, and recreate focus.

Know Your Values – Take time to reflect on what is really important to you. Understanding our moral and social values makes a big difference in perspective.

Knowing where we stand in terms of how we treat other people, what constitutes lying and cheating, and thinking about how we can prevent harm and do good provides us with a proactive mindset – we generally think of mental toughness as a response to some type of adverse conditions. Having a sound understanding of your moral values will help you navigate those situations before they become adverse.

Visualize: As we all know, the Stoics promoted negative imagery as a way to establish worth in the current moment as well as a way to get ready for unpleasant circumstances. Since we can now validate the procedure, visualization becomes an extremely useful mental tool for training both ourselves and other people. Imagine yourself navigating the scenarios that give you anxiety; try to mentally place yourself in the situation and practice managing it exactly the way you want to, whether or not you think you can pull it off. It's quite difficult to do better than our perception of ourselves, and The Little Train that Could was accurate.

Understand Your Threats – Since we know how our brains work in regard to visualization, we also know that we don't differentiate between threats, real or imagined. In my experience with athletes and Soldiers, we also don't distinguish between the three sources of threats. Physical threats, bodily harm, injury, or death; Social threats, which put either status, rank, or acceptance at risk; and emotional threats, which put our self-image, esteem, and feelings at risk. Reflect on what's really happening. Is this real, or imagined? What is at risk – physical, social, or emotional? Then ask yourself, "Am I scared or am I hurt?"

Problem Solver vs. Answer Finder – It's an attitude/mindset thing. We don't do a very good job of teaching our kids to think anymore and with Google in everyone's pocket, our addiction to answers is limiting our thinking power and as a result, our ability to manage ambiguity. An aspect of mental toughness has to do with our ability to make predictions and estimate consequences. Learning to, and valuing, problem solving process helps center us in the moment and prepare for the future.

Practice – Expect and invite some stress into your life. Toughness isn't just about taking a beating or handling adversity. If we could isolate it from the rest of our world, it would be an imperviousness to adversity. Mental toughness is an action, it's not something we are born with or without. The more we prepare and practice the better – tougher – we'll be.

The Inner Strength of Marcus Aurelius

Marcus Aurelius, despite the turbulent obstacles of leading an empire, embodied inner strength via his constant dedication to Stoic ideas. His own thoughts, collected in the well-known book "Meditations," provide light on his incredibly strong character and remarkable resilience. Despite the political intricacies and demands of governing, Aurelius showed incredible fortitude by upholding the Stoic values and applying them as a framework for his choices and way of living.

Aurelius's advocacy of the Stoic school of thought emphasizes the value of cultivating a resilient mindset by accepting the unavoidable uncertainties in life. His thoughts frequently focused on how fleeting life is and urged acceptance of this impermanence of circumstances. In the midst of the tumult of his reign, Aurelius was able to preserve mental fortitude and serenity because he recognized the transient character of circumstances. The precepts of stoicism gave him comfort, guiding him to view obstacles as chances for progress rather than as causes of suffering.

Aurelius's inner power is demonstrated by his unshakable dedication to morality and virtue. Virtues including wisdom, courage, justice, and temperance were important to him and served as guiding principles in his judgments and deeds. Aurelius developed a resilience that allowed him to lead with humility, empathy, and reason by upholding these characteristics. His commitment to the Stoic philosophy is evidence of the perseverance that comes from leading a life governed by ideals that are independent of the outside world.

Chapter 23: The Role of Duty and Responsibility

Duty and duty are important factors that influence how people behave and develop their moral compass and ethical behavior. A person's responsibilities and commitments, frequently dictated by moral, ethical, or personal values, are embodied in the concept of responsibility. It goes beyond simply following the law and delves farther into the areas of moral responsibility and dedication to a greater good. Accepting responsibility for one's conduct means that one understands the importance of what they do and how it affects the world.

Duty, however, functions within a context of moral agency and free will; it does not exist in a vacuum. Aurelius argued that people should carefully consider their responsibilities and make sure that their deeds are morally righteous and virtuous. He underlined the value of wisdom and discernment in realizing one's actual obligations and informing choices based on moral standards. In the end, the stoic view of obligation emphasizes how intrinsically linked it is to moral behavior and how much of an impact it has on forming personal integrity and maintaining social harmony.

Duty in Marcus Aurelius' Philosophy

The Stoic Emperor Marcus Aurelius tied his responsibility as a ruler and a Stoic practitioner together, emphasizing the importance of duty in his philosophy. For Aurelius, responsibility was an ethical imperative based on Stoic ideas as well as a social or political duty. He thought that people should carry out their duties with a feeling of moral obligation and a dedication to the greater good.

Throughout his meditations, which are collected in "Meditations," Aurelius frequently considered his obligations as an emperor. He believed that the universe's divine order and fate had given him the responsibility of being a leader. He recognized the gravity of his duties and emphasized the need of leading and serving with moral rectitude, equity, and kindness. His feeling of duty was derived from the Stoic virtues, which led him to rule with compassion, knowledge, and justice.

Aurelius's Stoic philosophy emphasized the cultivation of inner virtues and moral principles as a fundamental duty of every individual. He believed that everyone had a duty to practice self-discipline, cultivate wisdom, and live in accordance with virtue. Aurelius taught that embracing one's duty involved introspection, self-improvement, and adherence to ethical values. He advocated for personal responsibility, urging individuals to fulfill their duties not out of compulsion but as an expression of their moral integrity.

Within Aurelius's philosophy, the Stoic notion of obligation encompassed not only political and personal spheres but also a wider duty to humanity. He emphasized how every person is a member of a greater community and how interconnected they are. Aurelius thought that one's responsibility included making a constructive contribution to society, demonstrating empathy, and advancing the welfare of the group as a whole. His ideology promoted a sense of responsibility that went beyond self-interest and was intended to promote peaceful interpersonal relationships.

Balancing Personal and Public Responsibilities

It is a complex endeavor that requires a careful blending of self-awareness, ethical judgment, and social commitment to balance personal and public responsibilities. People work hard to meet their personal commitments to themselves, their families, and their own development. This includes a number of things, such taking care of one's physical and mental health, pursuing one's own goals, and fostering interpersonal relationships. People live in a social environment and have obligations to their local, national, and even international communities.

Chapter 24: The Universality of Stoic Philosophy

The continuing universality of stoic philosophy is rooted in its emphasis on universal human qualities that cut across cultural, geographic, and chronological boundaries. Fundamentally, stoicism provides a practical way of living by emphasizing values that are applicable to all cultures. Through the millennia, its lessons on morality, personal virtue, and perseverance in the face of hardship have remained relevant and appealing to people looking for direction in navigating the complexity of life.

One of the key pillars of Stoicism is the distinction between what lies within an individual's control and what doesn't. This concept speaks universally to the human desire for agency and autonomy in shaping one's life. The Stoic emphasis on focusing energy and attention on internal states, such as one's thoughts, values, and actions, rather than fixating on external circumstances, resonates with people across cultures who seek inner peace and emotional resilience.

The focus on virtue ethics in Stoic philosophy offers a moral framework that cuts across cultural divides. Characteristics such as bravery, fairness, moderation, and wisdom are widely cherished in many cultures, faiths, and philosophical systems. People seeking guidance in moral decision-making, regardless of cultural ties, will find common ground in the Stoic emphasis on acquiring these virtues as a means of leading a good and meaningful life.

Stoicism's teachings on the acceptance of life's transience, impermanence, and the inevitability of change are universally relatable experiences. The recognition of the ephemeral nature of life and the Stoic call to embrace impermanence resonate with individuals from various cultural backgrounds who grapple with the uncertainties and fluctuations of existence. This universal aspect of human experience forms a basis for Stoic teachings to resonate deeply across cultures, offering solace and guidance in navigating life's unpredictabilities.

Zeno, the Stoic founder, believed that "living in agreement with nature" leads to a smooth flow of life (euroiabiou), which forms the basis of Stoic philosophy. Clenthes, a pupil of Zeno, was the second head of the Stoics and added the final clause, "with nature" (tephusei; literally, "according to," kata phusin).The Stoics perceived a world-city of people who were linked to it and to each other as social beings and as a fully material reality that was permeated with reason and purpose. Zeno had challenged his students to get to the place where everything they did was in "harmonious accord with each man's guiding spirit and the will of the one who governs the universe."

It was no coincidence that Zeno was the first philosopher to treat duty (*kathekon*), our responsibility to act appropriately in our given roles in family and society, as a central concern. It was also a direct result of his teachings that we were required to engage in public life until we are unable to do so.

Happiness Is Found in Virtue Alone—It Depends on Our Values and the Decisions We Make While there was much disagreement among the early Stoics regarding many specifics, they all agreed that the only path to happiness for humans was to pursue virtue (arete, or human excellence), which required controlling our impulses, desires, and aversions to better align with the four cardinal virtues of temperance (sophrosune), courage (andreia), justice (dikaiosune), and practical wisdom (phronesis).

Put simply, morality is the software we are all supposed to be following; it just so happens to be the ideal operating system for humans to navigate the world. The numerous ancillary qualities that are related to these four primary virtues.

We cannot complain or place blame on anyone else.

The stoics held that there was a single, rational self. They accepted responsibility for upholding that unity and would never condone thinking along the lines of "the devil made me do it" or assigning blame or accountability to any other party. Among the Stoics, the towering genius Posidonius stands out for having altered the psychology of the Stoics to better explain the irrational forces he witnessed tearing apart great leaders like Pompey in his own time. As Posidonius stated, "to live contemplating the truth and order of the universe and promoting it as much as possible, one must design one's life."

We Don't Control External Events, We Only Control Our Thoughts, Opinions, Decisions and Duties

When we keep externals in the proper perspective, we gain a steadiness (*eustatheia*) that helps us along life's way. In the real world, we all have things we need and duties and obligations that arise from our family, relationships, and vocations. Zeno was the first to divide these externals into what he called "preferred and dispreferred indifferents." What he meant is that while they don't have intrinsic moral value, they form a kind of second class of value that is an important part of our lives—things like health and wealth are to be preferred over sickness and poverty, and if we are lucky enough to have them they can be a benefit to us and others as we pursue a virtuous life.

Stoicism and Its Relevance Across Cultures

Stoicism's enduring relevance transcends cultural boundaries due to its universal principles and practical wisdom that resonate with individuals across various cultures and eras. Its emphasis on inner resilience, ethical living, and understanding the human condition aligns with fundamental aspects of human experience, making it applicable across diverse cultural contexts. The Stoic philosophy's core teachings, originating from ancient Greece and Rome, have found resonance and adaptation in different cultural traditions and societies worldwide.

Across cultures, Stoicism's teachings on virtue ethics and the pursuit of wisdom resonate deeply with notions of moral conduct, integrity, and personal excellence. The Stoic emphasis on virtues like courage, justice, temperance, and wisdom aligns with ethical values cherished in diverse cultural settings. These virtues provide a moral compass that guides individuals toward leading principled and meaningful lives, fostering a sense of purpose and direction regardless of cultural differences.

Moreover, Stoicism's adaptability and openness to interpretation have allowed it to integrate seamlessly into various philosophical, religious, and cultural traditions worldwide. While its origins lie in ancient Western philosophy, Stoic principles have found parallels and integration with Eastern philosophies, mindfulness practices, and even modern psychological therapies. This adaptability underscores Stoicism's cross-cultural relevance, demonstrating its capacity to resonate with individuals seeking guidance for navigating life's complexities across diverse cultural landscapes.

Timeless Lessons from Marcus Aurelius

Through his thoughts, the Roman Emperor and Stoic philosopher Marcus Aurelius left behind a priceless legacy that has inspired generations of people. His writings, which were frequently written during times of conflict and personal hardship, contain insightful observations that are still relevant and useful in today's world.

Accepting difficulty as a natural part of life is one of the most important lessons to be learned from Marcus Aurelius' meditations. He stresses the value of resilience in the face of adversity and exhorts people to accept and adjust to life's unavoidable setbacks. This timeless lesson serves as a reminder to view challenges as chances for personal growth and development rather than as impassable barriers.

The core of the Stoic Emperor's philosophy is to concentrate on what we can influence. Introspection and self-reflection are often urged by Marcus Aurelius, who promotes control over one's thoughts, deeds, and emotions. His lessons stress that although events outside of our control may be uncontrollable, we still have power over our reactions, attitudes, and impressions. This ageless lesson gives people the ability to focus their energies on developing morality and inner strength rather than letting outside forces devour them.

Focus on your mind, not the outside events.

"Everything is interwoven, and the web is holy; none of its parts are unconnected. They are composed harmoniously, and together they compose the world. One world, made up of all things. One divinity, present in them all. One substance and one law—the logos that all rational beings share. And one truth… If this is indeed the culmination of one process, beings who share the same birth, the same logos. " [Meditations, book VII].

One of the most important convictions is the Stoic worldview. They believed that the world is organized rationally and coherently. More specifically, the all-pervading force called "logos" rules the world and constantly strives to achieve its goal.

All events are determined by the Logos and follow an unbreakable chain of cause and effect. Aurelius was deeply convinced that Stoic philosophy shows that human life, despite its apparent vanity, has a very definite sense. And all the hurtful events and changes in the world constitute a one, uniform process that realizes a greater goal.

Attitude is foundational.

"The things you think about determine the quality of your mind. Your soul takes on the color of your thoughts." [Meditations, book VII]

Aurelius believed in the driving force of thoughts. He was clear that thoughts, both from an individual and a general perspective, influence the shape of the world.

Following stoic philosophy, Marcus Aurelius was deeply convinced of the purposefulness and the rationality of the universe. But what reveals that the rational side of the universe is so-called "pneuma", a divine force that permeates everything.

He therefore held the view that everything is interconnected, emphasizing the relationship between a man and the cosmos in particular. However, it turns out that a man's strong connection within himself is more significant when it comes to the caliber of his thoughts.

The emperor philosopher believed that people are connected to both the outside world and their own self. Our life quality is a direct result of the connection between our mind and thoughts. Thus, he came to believe that thinking more positively is preferable to thinking negatively.

Happiness is a skill you can develop.

"But true good fortune is what you make for yourself. Good fortune: good character, good intentions, and good actions." [Meditations, book V]

Aurelius believed that people have more influence over their overall happiness and quality of life than they may realize. He leaves events and circumstances beyond of his control and deals with practicing happiness on his own, as he has power over it.

The lessons imparted by the Stoic Emperor regarding the value of upholding moral principles and pursuing virtue are still relevant in our times. He highlights the foundation of a purposeful and happy existence being the development of qualities such as justice, courage, temperance, and wisdom. Integrity, moral rectitude, and ethical behavior are emphasized by Marcus Aurelius as the most important virtues for guiding people through the challenges of contemporary life.

Marcus Aurelius' profound insights into the nature of humanity and the interconnectedness of all beings transcend temporal and cultural boundaries. His reflections underscore the universal capacity for reason and the shared experiences that unite humanity. His emphasis on empathy, compassion, and the acknowledgment of our common humanity resonates with individuals seeking deeper connections and understanding in a diverse and interconnected world. The Stoic Emperor's teachings on the importance of self-awareness and introspection continue to inspire contemporary practices such as mindfulness, cognitive-behavioral therapy, and self-improvement methodologies. His emphasis on disciplined self-examination and the quest for self-improvement serves as a timeless guide for personal development and growth in the modern era.

The insight of Marcus Aurelius includes an understanding of the impermanence of existence and the certainty of change. His thoughts on the transient nature of life and the transience of material belongings inspire people to let go of earthly ties and embrace a deeper feeling of fulfillment that comes from living morally and with inner qualities.

Printed in Great Britain
by Amazon

41484023R00079